QUÉBEC

QUÉBEC

A PHOTOGRAPHIC ROAD TRIP THROUGH CANADA'S BEAUTIFUL PROVINCE

MATHIEU DUPUIS

NATIONAL GEOGRAPHIC

WASHINGTON, D.C.

CONTENTS

INTRODUCTION

GREW UP IN A PART OF SOUTHWESTERN QUÉBEC where beautiful, untamed nature was but a few minutes from my home. Within this region of 22,143 square miles (57,349 sq km)—the fourth largest in the province of Québec—there are almost as many lakes, rivers, and marshes as there are inhabitants. It is called Abitibi-Témiscamingue, Algonquin for "where the waters separate" and "deep lake"—both for the watershed of the magnificent rift valley Lake Timiskaming and the lake itself, which is 709 feet (216 m) deep in some places.

Inasmuch as our childhood shapes who we become as adults, it is no surprise that nature photography became my passion. Those open spaces at my fingertips, combined with my Algonquin roots, inspired me to explore and discover. As a teenager I seized every opportunity to venture into places that seemed untouched by humans. I dreamed of retracing the paths of the *coureurs des bois*—expert woodsmen and trappers who had canoed up the local rivers centuries before, in search of furs for the fur trade.

Topics for my bedtime reading ranged from survival in the woods to paddling technique. Outdoors I would spend long hours on the region's lakes and rivers in my Explorer canoe, sometimes paddling against the current, or portaging across forbidding rapids in search of good lighting and new discoveries. When not on the water I would climb the nearby mountains to sit upwind on some peak, topographic map in hand, contemplating the endless horizon.

After a few years I felt compelled to take my camera and explore Québec beyond my backyard. I took the next step, specializing in travel and landscape photography. Now, some 20 years later, being on the

OPPOSITE: The legendary de Havilland Beaver bush plane skims the Grande River, a main source of hydroelectric power in Québec, in James Bay.

PREVIOUS PAGES: Centre-du-Québec is luminous from dawn to dusk (pages 2 and 3). Enthroned on Cap Diamant above Old Québec City, Château Frontenac hotel (page 4) sits above an archaeological site for the Château St. Louis, built for the first French governors in 1620.

road and in the air is part of my daily routine; this lifestyle is my passion. With wonder I discover the world, little by little, photograph by photograph.

But Québec remains my home, my playground. When I spread a map across a table, I can associate an image or memory with nearly every place-name; nonetheless, the magic endures, and my love story with Québec continues as intensely as ever. Why? Simply because, when I least expect it, when I think I've seen and done everything, I am overcome with the feeling that every traveler seeks: I am transported elsewhere; I am abroad, even while at home.

Québec's range of cultural and geographical experiences is unique. Certainly it has its signature "must-sees"—Old Québec City, Percé Rock, Mont Tremblant—all rich and fascinating, with multiple personalities. Beyond these icons spread nearly 600,000 square miles (1.55 million sq km) of unique places—some reached by the province's 89,912 miles (144,700 km) of roads; others by chartered air, maritime cabotage, or ferry.

Because Québec was developed through its waterways, much of the population is concentrated along the magnificent St. Lawrence. The province's first channel of exploration and commerce, the St. Lawrence

ABOVE: The author photographs a wintry St. Lawrence River panorama: Here the tides have crushed river ice against the rocky shore.

and its tributaries enabled European explorers to press into the Canadian backcountry and have helped define the character of Québec's regions.

The first inhabitants of Québec were Aboriginal peoples, followed by French explorers led by Samuel de Champlain in 1608, then by intermittent British and other newcomers. The early immigrants took up residence along the St. Lawrence close to the native peoples, intermingling over time. Today, while integrated, each group retains its individualistic culture.

Through my photography I have had the privilege of sharing unforgettable moments with humble people who are passionate about

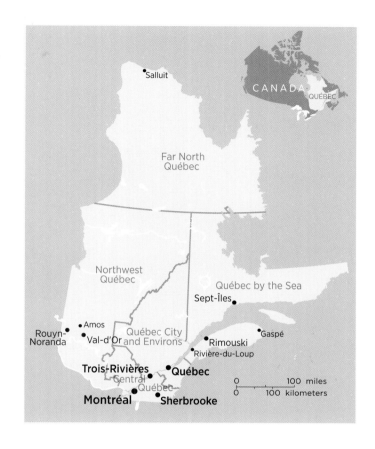

their separate regions. I have discovered these places sometimes with friends, sometimes alongside complete strangers who, through circumstances, became friends. People were always eager to help me find just the right place in just the right light to showcase their cherished home. These precious encounters give my memories color and dimension. While the images I capture on camera are embedded with the beauty of a place, they also evoke the warmth of the people who helped me see it through their eyes.

The Québec I know must be lived. If a picture is worth a thousand words, this book is filled with enticements for living your very own *aventure québécoise*.

QUÉBEC BY THE SEA

ALONG THE ST. LAWRENCE

FFECTIONATELY KNOWN as "the sea," the omnipresent St. Lawrence River shapes all aspects of life in maritime Québec. Its width varies greatly, with the river ranging from 0.5 to 3 miles (0.8–4.8 km) wide, while its estuary, 37 miles wide (59.5 km), broadens to 186 miles (299 km) in the gulf. No wonder that gazing upon the St. Lawrence is like contemplating the sea. At times the river is calm, rippled by a breeze that imparts a unique, satiny texture. In other moments it erupts and lashes out without warning. To live along this waterway, transporter of dreams and hopes, is to dwell in a world rich with history and legend. This corner of Québec saw the province's first encounters between European explorers and the Mi'kmaq and Innu First Nations. Today's museums and interpretive centers invite visitors to discover the richness and depth of Aboriginal cultures. The four regions that define this part of the province — Côte-Nord, the Îles-de-la-Madeleine (Magdalen Islands), Gaspésie (Gaspé Peninsula), and Bas Saint-Laurent — are choice areas for those who enjoy gazing toward the horizon. These places continue to evolve symbiotically with the river, its natural wonders, and its extraordinary diversity. No one who travels Route 138 along the river's north shore or Route 132 along the south shore remains untouched by the splendid, ever changing scenery. Each area's enticements are an invitation to stay awhile and discover its secrets.

Sept-Îles

Harrington Harbour

FORILLON NATIONAL PARK Cap Gaspé

Tadoussac   Sainte-Flavie

Île du Havre aux Maisons

Rivière-du-Loup

La Grave

Montréal

OPPOSITE: Dawn near the village of Les Boules highlights boulders that dot the banks of the St. Lawrence in this area.

PREVIOUS PAGES: Sculpted by the forces of nature over thousands of years, the unique geologic structure of Percé Rock is a majestic part of the rich landscape of Gaspésie.

CÔTE-NORD
AT THE END OF THE WORLD

Vast expanses, whales, and Route 138 mark the Côte-Nord region. One drives endless kilometers through vast nature and then arrives at ... "the end of the world." Spread out like beads on a rosary, villages can be reached only by boat or plane. Along the coast, whales breach. Experiencing Côte-Nord is discovery of its unique environment, enriched by the Innu First Nation and French culture and history. It is also the village of Natashquan, birthplace of renowned Quebecois singer-songwriter and poet Gilles Vigneault (born 1928), who speaks poetically of his beloved Québec.

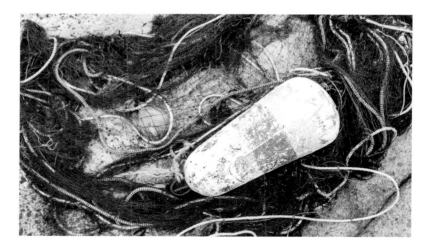

LEFT: Île d'Anticosti is a trove of stunning natural wonders. After hiking through a canyon with towering 295-foot (90 m) cliffs, visitors reach the breathtaking Vauréal Falls.

ABOVE AND FOLLOWING PAGES: Côte-Nord is a popular spot for commercial and recreational fishing. Gilles Monger (page 16), of Tête-à-la-Baleine, is a principal turned lobsterman. In Harrington Harbour (page 17) walkways connect the buildings.

LEFT: The *Calou*, a wooden trawler that ran aground at Pointe Ouest on Île d'Anticosti, is a reminder of the fate of sailors who have been shipwrecked here.

ABOVE: The Pointe Ouest lighthouse keeper's home is now a countryside inn without electricity. Staying here is a memorable historic experience on mystical Anticosti.

LEFT: The Île d'Anticosti riverbed at low tide, lined by the colorful houses of Port-Menier village, creates a spectacular sight, as do the deer that graze nearby.

ABOVE: The Mingan Archipelago—a chain of some 40 islands, including a national park reserve—is famed for its enormous limestone monoliths sculpted by the sea.

ABOVE: These stones represent the geologic history of Côte-Nord. As glaciers cut grooves into the rock, these valuable sediments were left behind.

OPPOSITE: A trail crosses an Innu tepee camp near Rivière-au-Tonnerre, in the Minganie area. From here the Thunder River drops 164 feet (50 m) in a raging waterfall.

FOLLOWING PAGES: The bustling port of the Sept-Îles archipelago (pages 24–25), just 6 miles (9.6 km) across, has 14 wharves and an airport zone, with helipad. Pointe des Monts Lighthouse (page 26), a national heritage site, delivers stunning, vertigo-inducing views from the top. From Pointe des Monts (page 27), which extends 6.8 miles (11 km) into the St. Lawrence, whales are a common sight.

OPPOSITE: Poised at the confluence of the St. Lawrence River and Saguenay Fjord and surrounded by mountains, the ancient village of Tadoussac's natural wonders amaze visitors at each hour of the day. Without a doubt, whale-watching is one of the major draws of this tourist hot spot.

ABOVE RIGHT: Emmanuel Sandt-Duguay, a snow-crab fisherman in Portneuf-sur-Mer, heads out on a morning voyage among the ice floes on the St. Lawrence. Once the crab boat has reached the open sea, the ritual begins: The cages are hauled up, the crabs are collected in a giant tub and sorted, and then the cages go back into the water. The expedition takes hours, but the view the fishermen take in is striking, even in the cold winter morning.

BELOW RIGHT: Whale-watching is almost an obsession for tourists heading to Côte-Nord. This whale, spotted by a hopeful group off the coast of Les Escoumins near the Innu village of Essipit, will satisfy the innate human fascination with these stunning animals, the largest cetaceans in the St. Lawrence River.

GASPÉSIE

A RUGGED, WINDSWEPT REGION

The *tour de la Gaspésie*, the legendary tour of the Gaspé Peninsula —a 550-mile (885 km) loop along Route 132—instantly evokes the sea, the mountains, and postcard icon Percé Rock. Yet there is more: Chaleur Bay, containing some of the warmest saltwater north of Virginia, in the United States; stunning parklands; the Chic-Choc Mountains; salmon fishing; and the Gaspésie culture waiting to be discovered. Museums and interpretive centers tell of the fishermen's way of life and Aboriginal traditions.

LEFT: An enormous world of nature unfolds during a stroll along the shore of Gaspé Bay in Forillon National Park, which brims with natural treasures in every season.

ABOVE: Gîte du Mont-Albert is a mountain hotel in the heart of Gaspésie National Park. Cloaked in fog, Mont Albert, one of the Chic-Choc Mountains, might be mistaken for a giant towering above the land.

LEFT: A heritage site in Forillon National Park, the Hyman & Sons General Store demonstrates how shops once sold goods, from porcelain tableware to medicines. One exhibit features the importance of the cod industry at the turn of the 20th century.

ABOVE AND FOLLOWING PAGES: In Forillon National Park, Blanchette House is testament to the early 20th-century lifestyle of fishing families. Forillon supports harmonious cohabitation between bears (page 35) and visitors, requiring visitors to follow strict rules. Cap Bon-Ami (page 34) is untamed wilderness, with maritime vistas frequented by whales.

"THE SEABIRD SANCTUARY IS WELL KNOWN; HOWEVER, MANY OTHER SPOTS WITHIN A CLOSE DISTANCE ARE WONDERFUL SOURCES FOR BIRDERS AND NATURE LOVERS."

—JOHN WISEMAN, PERCÉ RESIDENT AND

ARTIST-NATURALIST ON GASPÉSIE

This foggy morning vista in the shadow of Percé Rock is a common sight in the spring. Here fishermen head out to sea to drop and haul up crab pots.

Île Bonaventure hosts one of the largest colonies of northern gannets in the world.
These slender, streamlined birds can dive at speeds of 62 miles (100 km) an hour into
deep waters for food.

Mont Saint-Joseph reveals the splendid topography of the region. The countryside is carved into forest, farmland, *barachois* (coastal lagoons), and open water. Together, they create a beautiful mosaic in Chaleur Bay.

LEFT: Mont Albert is one of the Chic-Choc Mountains. Its peak, a 7.7-square-mile (20 sq km) plateau, harbors an untamed wilderness that bends only to the wind and the cold. Here, an icy glaze sculpts the trees in unique shapes.

ABOVE: P-O and his father, Jean-Guy Lévesque, crab fishermen and backcountry skiing enthusiasts in the Chic-Chocs, skim across Mont Ernest-Laforce, with Mont Albert's hauntingly beautiful landscape behind them.

OPPOSITE: The Auberge de Montagne des Chic-Chocs perches 2,017 feet (615 m) above sea level in the heart of Matane Wildlife Reserve in Gaspésie National Park. Along with the mountains and diverse flora, the park's 23 square miles (60 sq km) shelter an untamed wilderness rich with moose, caribou, and white-tailed deer.

RIGHT: The Chic-Choc Mountains wait to greet lovers of the great outdoors. The diversity of the landscape, ranging from jagged, wooded ridges to deep, lush valleys, is exceptional. An excursion to Mont 780 takes visitors through a thick forest of ferns and offers a breathtaking, 360-degree panorama.

LEFT: The entrance to Gaspésie is Sainte-Flavie, a charming village on the banks of the St. Lawrence River. Mountains hug its borders.

ABOVE: Located between La Martre and Cap au Renard on Route 132, the stunning Bridal Veil Falls deserves a moment of admiration.

ÎLES-DE-LA-MADELEINE

SHAPED BY SEA AND WIND

Discovery of an insular lifestyle awaits visitors to the Magdalen Islands. The sea, the wind, the sand, the red sandstone cliffs, the brightly colored houses shape the scenery. The local Madelinot dialect reflects the island's history and cultural depth, influenced by First Nations, French, and Acadian vocabulary and accents. And there is the special warmth of the Madelinots themselves.

LEFT: Old Harry Beach on Grosse Île is typical of the rocky landscape of the Magdalen Islands. This treasured shoreline is composed of red sandstone bluffs sculpted by the erosive forces of nature over millennia.

ABOVE: A shipwreck, guardian of the history of the sea and its temper, rests on the shore near Old Harry.

47

LEFT: This island sand dune near Havre-aux-Maisons is a dreamland. Dunes make up 60 percent of the Magdalen Islands shoreline. They are essential to maintaining ecological balance and add their own brand of beauty to the archipelago.

ABOVE: The brightly colored houses on Havre-aux-Maisons are not constructed in rows in neighborhoods, but are scattered across the terrain, built out of the path of the prevailing winds.

FOLLOWING PAGES: Nature and humanity have joined forces to create this lupine-inspired landscape in Havre-Aubert, a member of the Association of the Most Beautiful Villages of Québec.

ABOVE: This enormous rock at the end of Île d'Entrée is a solitary feature on the open water. The island itself is home to about 100 residents year-round. The only island not connected to others in the chain, its population is mainly of Scottish and Irish descent.

OPPOSITE: Known as the lobster capital of Québec, Île de la Grande Entrée hosts some 100 fishing boats and is home to a fish-processing plant. Blue mussels are farmed in the bay, with crabs, scallops, and mackerel caught as well.

FOLLOWING PAGES: The hills of the Chemin des Échoueries on Île du Havre aux Maisons overlook the impressive cliffs of Buttes Pelées. For some, they serve as landmarks on the water. For others, they cut the wind and invite daredevils to scale them and discover the distant horizon. The cliffs subtly transform the scenery over the course of the days and seasons, depending on the changing light.

OPPOSITE: Kayaking is a great way to explore cliffs, lagoons, sand dunes, and inaccessible beaches from the water.

ABOVE RIGHT: The fishing center of the Magdalen Islands, Étang-du-Nord is always bustling, thanks to its many outdoor activities. An annual art symposium brings together painters inspired by the beauty of the archipelago.

BELOW RIGHT: Reality, or just an illusion? This scene can easily be mistaken for a real-life photograph at twilight in Étang-du-Nord. In his sculpture, artist Roger Langevin has done justice to the strength and solidarity of fishermen, represented by the rope that unites them. This masterpiece honors the people who ply the trade, sometimes against the wind and the sea.

FOLLOWING PAGES: Around the Magdalen Islands, lobster fishing is regulated in order to maintain lobster population numbers (page 58). For example, regulations control the minimum size of the lobster that may be caught and the maximum number of traps that may be dropped (page 59). Fishermen are respectful of their quotas, and of this crustacean at the heart of a complex global industry. Daily ferry service between Souris, Prince Edward Island, and Cap-aux-Meules, Magdalen Islands, offers a relaxing five-hour trip each way (pages 60–61). In summer, a week-long cruise of the islands leaves from Montréal.

TRAVEL DIARY

This sudden clearing of the heavens, only moments before the last ray of sunlight disappears, is a gift. Here I stand, camera at the ready, at the very moment the elements unleash themselves to offer one of the most beautiful spectacles I have seen in a long time. I know from experience that this kind of light is fleeting—so every shot counts. One hand on the umbrella diffuser and the other on the camera, I release the shutter rapidly so as not to miss a thing. People wander out on balconies and patios to witness this extraordinary sunset. Then, as quickly as the colors appeared, they disappear. And gray dominates. An older couple out for a stroll stops. The man, with a knowing smile, says: "My dear young man, I have lived here all my life and this is the first time I have seen La Grave so spectacularly beautiful. Surely you must be living a good life to be present at this very moment."

A walk at sunset along La Grave, the first settlement on Île du Havre-Aubert, is an appointment with the history and architecture of the Magdalen Islands—as well as one of nature's beautiful spectacles.

BAS SAINT-LAURENT

WHERE WATER AND SUN MEET

"Sheer diversity" is the definition of the unforgettable Lower St. Lawrence region. Agricultural countryside lies amid large hills where picturesque villages nestle. Spectacular maritime views unfold along the coastline, with its myriad enticing activities: whale-watching; island-hopping to Île Verte (Green Island) with its legendary 19th-century lighthouse—Québec's oldest; water sports; and cycling or motorbiking along thematic routes.

LEFT: Across verdant farmland and the north shore of the St. Lawrence River, the mountains of Charlevoix tower in the distance. This landscape is characteristic of the Kamouraska area of Bas Saint-Laurent.

ABOVE: Lac Témiscouata National Park is a paddling paradise. The Chemins d'Eau, more than 186 miles (300 km) of waterways crisscrossing the region, invite exploration by kayak or canoe.

LEFT: Bic National Park features a wide range of natural habitats, from salt marshes to forests. Combined with the park's mountains, such as Pic Champlain on the horizon, the views in Bic are unique.

ABOVE: Winter brings its own beauty to the St. Lawrence River shoreline. The last light of day punctuates this snowshoe excursion.

OPPOSITE: A brightly painted home in winter complements the natural landscape of snow, sky, and water.

ABOVE RIGHT: Among the many magnificent views of the St. Lawrence coastline are these hills along the horizon near Notre-Dame-du-Portage. A popular tourist location with sought-after holiday resorts, the area embraces the beauty and character of its river. Exploring the St. Lawrence islands by guided tour or cruise ship makes for an unparalleled encounter with wildlife from seals to great blue herons.

BELOW RIGHT: Kamouraska has been a hot spot for eel fishing for three centuries. At low tide, the landscape transforms to reveal the measures taken to capture this quick and elusive fish. Starting in April, fishermen use pickets and nets to set up their fishing weirs along grooves in the riverbank. At high tide the eels swim into the weirs; at low tide the fishermen collect their catch.

FOLLOWING PAGES: At sunset, Mother Nature burnishes the landscape with last light. Welcome to Île aux Lièvres. Located between Saint-Siméon and Rivière-du-Loup on the St. Lawrence River, this island is composed of numerous rocky outcrops and riverbeds. Deciduous and coniferous trees fill the island, leaving little room for shrubs and bushes favored by the many hares on the island. This place is a paradise for animals in the estuary, and for people who love the tranquil splendor of nature.

OPPOSITE: The Îles du Pot à l'Eau-de-Vie ("brandy pot islands") are visited by many species of seabird, including auks and razorbills. During nesting season, access to trails is limited to promote sustainable tourism. The historic lighthouse rises above the craggy shore. Legend holds that during Prohibition bootleggers' smuggled alcohol was hidden here, giving the islands their name.

ABOVE RIGHT: Among the diverse kinds of wildlife of the islands, a seal blends into the rocky landscape.

BELOW RIGHT: A razorbill flies toward the islands' steep cliffs. A relative of the auk, these birds are at home in the air and on the water. On land they are clumsy; they rarely walk, and prefer to take flight from their cliffside nests.

FOLLOWING PAGES: The islands' rocky cliff faces welcome vast colonies of birds, mainly common murres, a species of auk. These birds spend most of their time at sea, returning to land mainly to raise their young. At rest on the rocks, they stand proudly upright, elegant as royalty.

LEFT: A variety of trails running through Lac Témiscouata National Park offer challenging treks for experienced hikers as well as winding paths for others who want to discover the verdant landscape at a more leisurely pace.

ABOVE: The eastern point of Île aux Lièvres ("hares island") melts into the horizon. Accessible only by passenger boat, it is a camping and hiking paradise with some 28 miles (45 km) of trails of varying difficulty.

THE QUÉBEC TRAVELER

1-DAY ADVENTURE: ÎLES-DE-LA-MADELEINE | Defined by rugged red sandstone cliffs, this archipelago in the Gulf of St. Lawrence is accessible by air or sea. Spend the day at La Grave on Île du Havre-Aubert. This pebble beach—site of the islands' first settlement—offers cafés and restaurants, shops, museums, a theater, and even an aquarium. If you visit in early August, don't miss the Festival Acadien, an annual celebration of Acadian culture that includes boat-building contests and fireworks displays.

2-DAY ADVENTURE: GASPÉSIE | Located within easy reach of Québec City, this windswept and sparsely populated peninsula warrants a two-day visit. Begin in Forillon National Park, where nature and history mingle. Take the easy La Taïga trail to a blind to observe some of the park's 246 bird species, or follow 2.5-mile (4 km) Les Graves past the Cap Gaspé lighthouse to Land's End, where the Chic-Choc Mountains meet the Atlantic Ocean. On day two, have an early breakfast in Percé before catching a boat cruise to remote Île Bonaventure et du Rocher Percé National Park, site of legendary Percé Rock, the haunting limestone arch rising from the Gulf of St. Lawrence. Disembark and hike across Île Bonaventure to see one of the largest colonies of northern gannets in the world.

3-DAY ADVENTURE: CÔTE-NORD | Begin with a visit to the Mingan Archipelago, which stretches some 93 miles (150 km) along the north shore of the Gulf of St. Lawrence and encompasses nearly a thousand islands. A boat tour from Havre-Saint-Pierre will take you past colossal limestone outcroppings, captivatingly sculpted and dating back nearly 500 million years. Whales and seals inhabit these waters, while puffins, guillemots, razorbills, and other seabirds nest on the islands in spring. On the second day visit Sept-Îles and cruise the splendid islands that give the port town its name, searching the landscape for whales and other marine animals, as well as the migratory birds that populate the sanctuary on Île du Corossol. Or head to Île Grande Basque for a day of hiking or beachcombing. On the final day, join one of the popular whale-watching excursions that leave the historic village of Les Escoumins. Most tour operators guarantee a sighting, or the trip is free. It can be chilly on the water, so wear long pants and bring a sweater or jacket, a hat, and gloves. Afterward learn more about the area's cetaceans at the Marine Mammal Interpretation Centre in Tadoussac.

Casse-croûte du Pêcheur ("fisherman's snack") is an essential stop at the Sept-Îles fishing harbor. The unique decor of the restaurant is outshone only by the fresh taste of the seafood and the fresh sea air.

QUÉBEC CITY & ENVIRONS

BRIMMING WITH HISTORY

TO FLY OVER the St. Lawrence River is to gain a unique perspective on Québec. Continuing south from Côte-Nord, one crosses the Saguenay River as it flows into the St. Lawrence, in the Saguenay–Lac Saint-Jean region. A glance to the northwest reveals the spectacular outline of the Saguenay's uncommon fjord—the southernmost in North America. Along the fjord's western edge, the rounded mountains of the Laurentian Massif rise suddenly. The mesmerizing aerial view of this region, called Charlevoix, takes in hillside villages, the majestic St. Lawrence, the high relief of the Laurentian Plateau, and valleys concealing stretches of tundra carved by glaciers some two million years ago.

On the other side of the St. Lawrence, called la Côte-du-Sud ("the south coast"), the Appalachian Mountains decline gently, giving way to Chaudière-Appalaches, a region of fertile green valleys around the Chaudière River. Flying toward Québec City along the river, the geographic importance of this urban hub becomes apparent. The name Québec comes from the Algonquin word for "where the river narrows"; aptly, the city stands guard over a passage where the St. Lawrence spans only 820 yards (750 m). Québec's oldest fort, La Citadelle, dominates the horizon. Beyond Québec City, the riverscape levels out in the Mauricie region. Here two islands separate the St. Maurice River, which pours into the St. Lawrence from the northwest, into three distinct channels. Running past Québec's second oldest city, Trois-Rivières, the St. Lawrence continues its sinuous trajectory southward.

SAGUENAY–LAC SAINT-JEAN

LAND OF GIANTS

They're called "the giants": the Saguenay Fjord, one of the world's longest, and Lake St. John, the largest populated lake in Québec. Together they comprise a vast region of stately and magnificent landscapes, with the fjord's immense cliffs sculpting the horizon. The region is known as the "land of blueberries," for its luscious fruit. A unique tour takes bikers around Lake St. John, on the 159-mile (256 km) Véloroute des Bleuets, the Blueberry Bikeway.

LEFT: Exploring Cap Trinité by water brings stunning views of this forested rock wall and its three plateaus overlooking Saguenay Fjord. On land, a footpath leads to the statue of Notre-Dame-du-Saguenay.

ABOVE: The *petite maison blanche*, or little white house, is famous for surviving the Saguenay flood of 1996. Now a museum, the house is an icon of Saguenay.

LEFT: A panorama of L'Anse-Saint-Jean from the Mille gazebo viewpoint shows the green-roofed covered bridge featured on the Canadian $1,000 bill.

ABOVE: Viewed from Anse de Tabatière, distant Saguenay Fjord—among the southernmost in the Northern Hemisphere—defines magnificent Saguenay Fjord National Park.

ABOVE: The port of call of La Baie is located on Ha! Ha! Bay, where cruise ships have stopped since 2008. Once a center for logging and paper industries, it is now a tourist site that welcomes visitors to the Saguenay region.

OPPOSITE: With an area of some 450 square miles (1,165 sq km), the city of Saguenay and environs offer museums, summer music and arts festivals, a stunning fjord, three national parks and a marine park, and the Blueberry Bikeway.

FOLLOWING PAGES: At 3,228 feet (984 m), Mont Valin dominates the landscape of Saguenay–Lac Saint-Jean. Monts Valin National Park receives some of the best natural snowfall in Québec—as much as 236 inches (600 cm) each year. Winter sports lovers like these are overjoyed by the opportunity to snowshoe through the park. The silence is brisk. The frozen landscape is a tranquil place, where only shadows move.

OPPOSITE: Scaling Mont Valin in search of its most beautiful views, or following its snowy trails, provides incomparable moments within its majestic natural environment. What a joy to spot this countryside cabin and relax by the fire.

RIGHT: Pallid light illuminates this spruce forest in Monts Valin National Park. At very high altitudes, the trees have adapted to the coldest climes and have a stunted appearance. For visitors, activities abound, including backcountry skiing. Under frost or snow, the view is breathtaking. Noted for the Vallée des Fantômes, or ghosts, the park indeed seems to be inhabited by ghosts, enchanting for hikers.

OPPOSITE: A member of the Montagnais community of Mashteuiatsh near Roberval in Lac Saint-Jean, Claude Boivin achieved his dream by creating a center of discovery and culture at Aventure Plume Blanche, where a unique experience gives visitors the opportunity to learn about Aboriginal cultures and traditions. For Boivin, the site of Aventure Plume Blanche is a symbol in itself: "This natural site conveys the essence of my own life, the origin of my creation. Walking across this territory is a source of energy and completeness that nourishes my spirit."

ABOVE RIGHT: The village of Val-Jalbert tells the story of the daily lives of a paper mill and its inhabitants. Following the decline of the mill, the village became a ghost town. Now restored, it is a historic site that draws many visitors.

BELOW RIGHT: The Aboriginal peoples of this region have a rich spiritual heritage that is expressed through traditional rituals, sacred objects, and symbolism. This moose skull hanging from a tree is an example. It is a symbol of respect toward the animal that nourished them.

CHARLEVOIX

AN ARTIST'S INSPIRATION

The beauty and history of Charlevoix have long been a source of artistic inspiration. Its winding roads, sheer cliffs, and villages tucked into valleys stole the heart of Swiss-born Canadian landscape artist René Richard (1895–1982), known for his semiabstract landscapes of the Canadian wilderness. Influenced by formal art study in France and time as a trapper alongside the Cree and the Inuit in northern Canada, Richard eventually settled in Baie-Saint-Paul. His colorful and luminous works are a precious legacy for Québec's cultural heritage.

LEFT: With homes and farms scattered across its slopes and valleys, this village, called Sainte-Irénée, offers a captivating view of the St. Lawrence River.

ABOVE: The *terroir*, or land, of Charlevoix is bountiful, and ideal for grazing cows. Exploring its local products and artisans is an experience for all the senses.

OPPOSITE: The waters off Port-au-Persil, a village near Saint-Siméon, are part of Saguenay–St. Lawrence Marine Park. With an area of 481 square miles (1,245 sq km), this park shelters an ecosystem where the waters of the St. Lawrence meet those of the Saguenay Fjord. This phenomenon fosters a rich biodiversity of aquatic flora and fauna. Five species of whales and more than 15 species of other marine mammals are known to frequent this area. Excursions are available to observe them in their natural habitat. Their appearance surprises watchers, while the rich tapestry of the sky brings breathtaking landscapes. This block of ice, a sample from the river, adds to the beauty of the park.

RIGHT: Port-au-Persil is a peaceful haven that lives by the ebb and flow of the tides. Located on bare rock, this small, white chapel was built in 1893. It has since become the symbol of Port-au-Persil. On calm evenings, belugas can be heard across the water.

"I WOULD SLEEP BY A WINDOW SO THAT MY LAST GOOD NIGHT CAME FROM THE MOON AND MY FIRST GOOD MORNING FROM THE SUN."

—FÉLIX LECLERC,

SINGER-SONGWRITER, AUTHOR, POET

This aerial shot of Hautes Gorges de la Rivière Malbaie National Park offers a stunning view of its geomorphology. Sculpted by ancient glaciers, the landscape is majestic.

With a vertical drop of 2,526 feet (770 m), Le Massif, located in Petite-Rivière-Saint-François, is the largest ski mountain not only in eastern Canada but east of the Rockies. The spectacular view of the St. Lawrence River adds to the joy of hitting the slopes, which are often covered with powder snow. At the summit, the snowpack can be 95 inches (240 cm).

Baie-Saint-Paul, on the north shore of the St. Lawrence River and close to Le Massif, follows the pace of the seasons. Inns, chalets, and holiday resorts give a warm welcome to tourists in a magical ambience. Birthplace of the world-renowned Cirque de Soleil, the town features art galleries, boutiques, and outdoor activities, including a popular 3.7-mile (6 km) drive down Le Massif to the St. Lawrence.

TRAVEL DIARY

GRAND JARDINS NATIONAL PARK

Grands Jardins National Park in the Charlevoix region boasts some of the area's most magnificent scenery. Major forest fires ravaged nearly 30 percent of the park in 1991 and again in 1999. The transformed landscape today provides astounding views of the burned "ancients."

At dawn, I walk along a muddy path by the light of my headlamp. Autumn comes slowly to this taiga environment—the zone between boreal forest and Arctic tundra. With every step, the mingled scent of earth and dead leaves fills my nostrils, giving me an olfactory rush.

The sun rises. The horizon brightens in a palette of luminous, golden colors. My clothes and surroundings are saturated with the morning dew. Suddenly my heart skips a beat, and then begins to race. A black bear is perched in a dead tree. She is at a safe distance, but the sight of her is enough to give me a rush of adrenaline—amplified when two little black heads pop up alongside her!

The cubs perch on their branches and take me in. I gently put down my backpack to extract my telephoto lens. I check the direction of the wind ... it is blowing my scent toward them. Already mama bear is sniffing the air. I take a few photos. The setting is superb, the light playing across the vegetation. I move a little closer. Then the maternal instinct kicks in and mama bear starts climbing down from the tree.

Numbering some 70,000 throughout Québec, black bears are especially partial to Grands Jardins National Park, where new-growth forests include plentiful berries and edible plants during summer months.

QUÉBEC CITY
TIMELESS

While Québec City has been a center of rule and culture since 1608, Île d'Orléans, the island of notable singer-songwriter Félix Leclerc (1914–1988), has its own allure. Surrounded by the St. Lawrence River, this early French colony has been called the "cradle of French civilization in North America." Known as the "garden of Québec," it is famous locally for its produce, wineries, and pastoral landscapes, and celebrated in a song by Leclerc: "[C]ome to the island; [a place of] forty-two thousand peaceful things to help you forget."

LEFT: The lighted Tourny Fountain, near Québec's Parliament Hill, blends harmoniously with the cityscape, complementing the Price Building, a jewel of Québec architecture, which dominates the horizon.

ABOVE: Cannons on the city fortifications of the Haute-Ville—Upper Town—and the Plains of Abraham are a reminder of the French-British battle here in 1759.

ABOVE: Valcartier's Hôtel de Glace, the Ice Hotel, offers an experience possible only in the ephemeral world of the north. Rooms built entirely from ice and snow have been adapted to ensure the comfort of those who dare to stay here.

OPPOSITE: Revitalized in the 1970s to reflect architecture and trades from as early as the 17th century, Petit Champlain is one of the most popular neighborhoods in Old Québec. One of its chief attractions, the famed 59-step Breakneck Stairs—dating from 1635—offers the best view of the area.

FOLLOWING PAGES: Rue Dalhousie, a mile-long (1.5 km) stroll along the base of Cap Diamant, enchants visitors with the stunning architecture of its buildings, its lively spirit, and proximity to the river and harbor. In the early dawn, a walk down this street is sublime. Later in the day, visitors often take the road to the Museum of Civilization and the Naval Museum of Québec at the city harbor.

LEFT: At 272 feet (83 m) in height, Montmorency Falls is an impressive natural wonder. Whether viewing it from the cable car, the suspension bridge, the 487-step panoramic staircase, or by flying along the 984-foot (300 m) zip line, the experience is staggering. When night falls, the waterfall's spectacular lighting gives visitors another view of its charm.

ABOVE: Numerous ancestral homes like this one along the Route de la Nouvelle-France showcase the European influence on the history of Québec. The route winds across 31 miles (50 km) of Côte de Beaupré and invites visitors to discover culture, agritourism, and treasures of architectural heritage.

OPPOSITE: Houses in neoclassical style, dating to the 19th century, give the village of Saint-Jean-de-l'Île-d'Orléans its charm. Home for many maritime pilots of the St. Lawrence River, its motto is *"La mer et la terre l'ont façonné—Built by the land and the sea."*

ABOVE RIGHT: An old cask on the side of the road invokes the island's winemaking heritage. Vineyards dot Île d'Orléans and can be explored by bike or by car in stunning surroundings. Guided tours and wine and cider tastings are available for visitors to fully appreciate the work of these artisans.

BELOW RIGHT: The quality and diversity of the local produce of Île d'Orléans have built the island's solid reputation in agritourism, helping the island fulfill its name as the "garden of Québec." Visitors will find their experiences enriched by good food and wine and local activities, which include visiting roadside fruit stands and craft shops and even driving a vintage truck through a farm orchard. In summer, strawberry and apple picking are popular pastimes here.

Classified as a historic monument since 1929, Notre Dame des Victoires Church is widely known as the cradle of French North America: It was built starting in the late 1680s on the ruins of the first outpost of Québec's founder, Samuel de Champlain. Dominating Place Royale in Old Québec's Haute-Ville, its three centuries of history are recounted by frescoes on either side of the altar.

The forested walls of the Jacques Cartier River Valley plunge a steep 1,804 feet (550 m) to their namesake river. As it winds through the valley, the rapid-rich river is a favorite destination for white-water rafters. Some 16 miles (26 km) of canoe routes and many land-based trails provide paths to discovery through the national park. In autumn, the yellow birch and maples blaze with color.

CHAUDIÈRE-APPALACHES

A PLACE FOR ALL SEASONS

At Québec's center and south along the St. Lawrence, the region's scenery astonishes with its diversity. The Appalachian Mountains forge sharp contrast against valleys and plains. In autumn, maple trees turn flamboyant yellow, fluorescent orange, brilliant red. Orchard fruits, goat cheese, beer brewed from Appalachian Mountain source water are products of the land. And there are the region's red deer. The sheer diversity of activities—from museum-hopping to winter snowmobiling—brings alive all the senses.

LEFT: Life is good in the town of Saint-Vallier-de-Bellechasse, whose period houses and endless stretches of green define the local landscape.

ABOVE: Discovering local products at one of the region's 130 gourmet stops is a delight to the senses.

FOLLOWING PAGES: Gary Cooper and Aagje Denys, owners of Cassiset Mélisse, produce milk and cheese from pasture-raised goats like the one at right.

LEFT: The St. Lawrence River estuary is dotted with islands. Visitors can board cruises to discover Grosse Île and the Isle-aux-Grues archipelago. The views are breathtaking.

ABOVE AND FOLLOWING PAGES: This window looks out onto the Corriveau family's century-old certified organic orchard in Saint-Vallier municipality. A cloud-washed horizon (pages 124-125) draws the eye to this wharf with its pleasure boats near Montmagny.

OPPOSITE: Vieux Lévis, the historic quarter of the city of Lévis, is best explored on foot to discover heritage buildings and architecture, welcoming sidewalk terraces, restaurants, and shops carrying high-quality products at every turn. Across the St. Lawrence, panoramic views of the river and Old Québec are astonishing in their beauty.

ABOVE RIGHT: The stunning pink color of this mountain, intensified by the sunrise, is a result of mining residue, a reminder of the rich geologic heritage of the Appalachian Mountains. The Thetford Mines Mineral and Mining Museum is a hidden gem of information on the history of asbestos, the lives of miners, and the region's development over the years.

BELOW RIGHT: Situated in the middle of the St. Lawrence River, Grosse Île was a quarantine station for immigrants entering Canada from 1832 to 1937. Today, Grosse Île and the Irish Memorial National Historic Site invite visitors to discover iconic buildings, like this one, and to learn about the immigrant experience.

MAURICIE
REGION OF CONTRASTS

Land of lakes, rivers, and boreal forests teeming with wildlife, Mauricie is a region of contrasts. Towns and villages dating from the 1600s recount their histories through local museums and interpreters. First Nations ancestral sites and early French pilgrimage sanctuaries, places of worship, and old forges all bear witness to a rich past. Myriad attractions, from La Mauricie National Park—home to the Laurentian Mountains—to the Forges du Saint-Maurice, birthplace of Canada's iron industry and a national historic site, reveal unique character and charm.

LEFT: Saint-Jean-des-Piles, known as the canoeing capital of Québec, is the main entry to La Mauricie National Park and popular for adventure tourism and fishing.

ABOVE: The historic past of Trois-Rivières is proudly on display at the Cathedral of the Assumption, built in 1852. This monument memorializes Monseigneur Louis-François Richer Laflèche, the second bishop of the diocese.

LEFT: Trois-Rivières' opulent houses, outdoor cafés, parks, and a promenade along the St. Lawrence River create the city's charm.

ABOVE: Mireille Dugré, co-owner of Jardins Dugré with her brother Simon, continues a three-generation family fruit and vegetable business.

FOLLOWING PAGES: The dome of the Ursulines Monastery dominates the rue des Ursulines in Old Trois-Rivières.

OPPOSITE: Number 52-6444 is part of a herd of 60 cattle roaming freely in green pastures and feeding off fresh grass and organic fodder grown on the F.X. Pichet farm in Champlain. There's no better source of delicious milk. It's a winning recipe for Michel Pichet and Marie-Claude Harvey, who own and operate the farm.

ABOVE RIGHT: Forges du Saint-Maurice National Historic Site shelters the remains of the first iron company in Canada. Installed in 1730, the forges burned here for more than 150 years. The site combines nature and culture.

BELOW RIGHT: Signs to paths for love and pleasure are part of the landscape in Mékinac Regional County Municipality—10 municipalities along the banks of the St. Maurice River. The area possesses a rural charm and thrives on local agricultural and forest resources. The wide-open spaces and lakes filled with fish are a paradise for outdoor enthusiasts. Outfitters are common here, and camping grounds and discovery trails are inviting.

FOLLOWING PAGES: Spring thaw in La Mauricie National Park presents landscapes typical of the Canadian Shield and the Laurentian hills, forests, and lakes. This majestic example of nature is protected by Parks Canada. It's an ideal destination for outdoor activities. Cycling paths, hiking trails, ski trails, and portage routes encourage visitors to explore the natural and cultural resources of the park.

THE QUÉBEC TRAVELER

PLANNING GUIDE FOR QUÉBEC CITY & ENVIRONS

1-DAY ADVENTURE: SAGUENAY–LAC SAINT-JEAN | Among the longest fjords in the world, 64-mile-long (103 km) Saguenay Fjord forms the heart of Fjord du Saguenay National Park. At the visitor center find the trailhead for the moderately difficult 4.7-mile (7.6 km) round-trip hike to the statue of the Virgin Mary, which has overlooked the Saguenay River since 1881. In the town of L'Anse-Saint-Jean, treat yourself at Pied d'Édouard's Nordic spa. Start with a steam bath followed by a dip in an ice-cold waterfall or snow, then relax in a resting area.

2-DAY ADVENTURE: CHARLEVOIX | Begin in the small hamlet of Port-au-Persil, wonderfully situated in a valley along the St. Lawrence River. Sample the local cider at the Cidrerie and browse the Poterie, which sells works by more than 50 ceramic artists. End the day in La Malbaie with dinner at elegant Restaurant le Patriarche. Or go casual at lively Maison du Bootlegger. Modified to hide illegal activity during Prohibition, this 19th-century farmhouse now offers tours and steak dinners. Spend the second day in Grands Jardins National Park, where you can rent a stand-up paddleboard and explore Lake Arthabaska. Small groups will enjoy a guided trip on a large rabaska canoe, made of tree bark. End in the town of Baie-Saint-Paul, birthplace of Cirque du Soleil and known for its art galleries. Themed self-guided tour maps are available at the tourist information center.

3-DAY ADVENTURE: QUÉBEC CITY | On day one, travel to Île d'Orléans, one of the first regions in Québec colonized by the French. Just a 15-minute drive from Québec City, this island full of wineries and farms, historic buildings, and specialty shops is best explored by car. Next, visit Montmorency Falls, gateway to Côte de Beaupré. Walking trails and a gondola provide spectacular views of the 272-foot-high (83 m) falls, the St. Lawrence River, and Île d'Orléans. Spend day two in Old Québec, established as a French colonial outpost in 1608. Easily traversed on foot, the compact old town—a UNESCO World Heritage site—retains its historic atmosphere, with stone buildings lining narrow, winding streets. Start at the iconic Fairmont Le Château Frontenac, and then stroll the city, browsing boutique shops and cafés. The all-day hop-on, hop-off double-decker bus tour takes in 13 sites, including the Museum of Civilization and the Marché du Vieux Port, the city's largest farmers market. Reserve the third day for Portneuf. Drive or bike the Chemin du Roy, Canada's oldest highway, which follows the St. Lawrence River, linking Old Québec and Montréal. Or enjoy a round of golf at one of the region's popular courses.

Winter streets in the Petit Champlain neighborhood turn festive with the holidays. Québec residents and visitors alike revel in the wintry ambience.

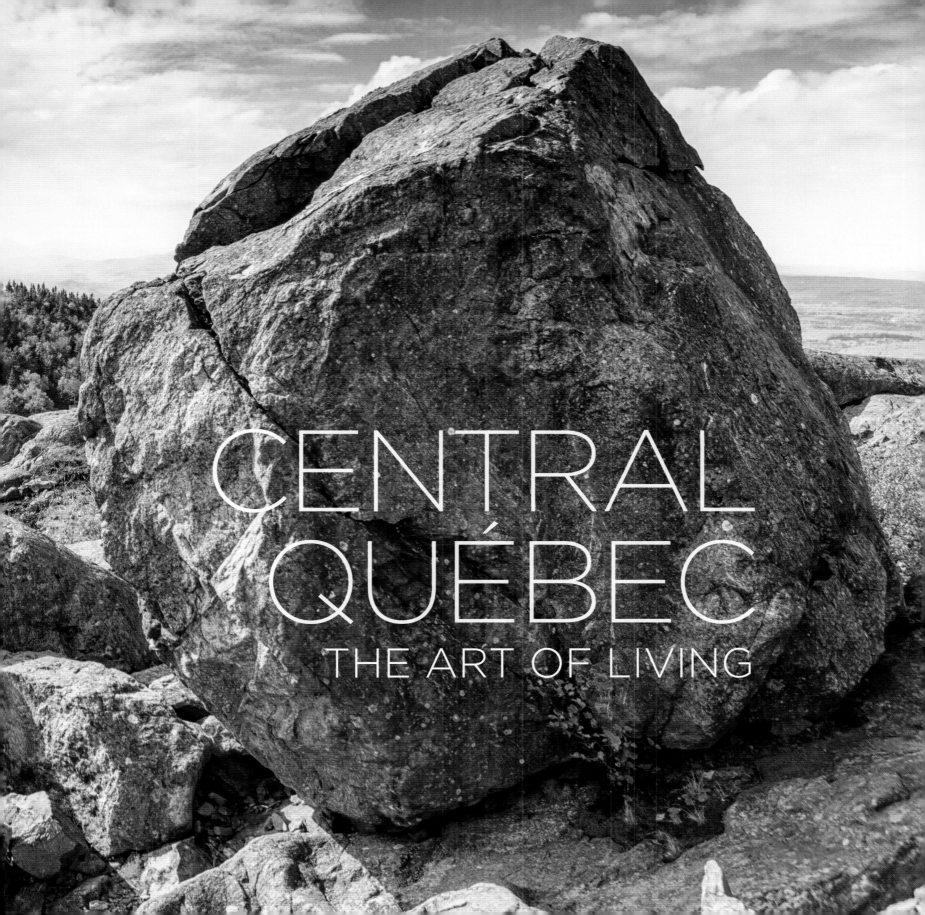

CENTRAL QUÉBEC

THE ART OF LIVING

FROM QUÉBEC CITY, the St. Lawrence widens into shallow Lake St. Pierre, a UNESCO biosphere reserve; then it narrows again and continues running southeast. On its southern bank lies the territory of Central Québec, with its first region, also called Centre-du-Québec, or Central Québec—a place of forests, pastoral villages, and rich, rolling farmland. Still farther south and to the west lie the regions of Cantons-de-l'Est (Eastern Townships) and Montérégie, respectively, with their stunning farmlands sculpted by the Monteregian Hills. Both share a boundary with the United States and have been shaped culturally by Aboriginal as well as French, English, and other immigrant influences.

As the St. Lawrence continues southward, Montréal, Québec's largest metropolis, looms on the horizon. At its heart lies the island of Montréal, with its 767-foot (234 m) Mont Royal. The predominantly French-speaking city is the cultural hub of Québec—a city of neighborhoods each with a distinctive character, boasting ethnic and cultural diversity. On the world stage, Montréal is synonymous with good living, as well as unparalleled art, music, film, food, and festivals including the Montréal International Jazz Festival. Best experienced on foot, the Quartier des Spectacles is the center of activity, complemented by numerous urban parks and seven nearby national parks.

North of Montréal lie the Laurentides to the west and Lanaudière to the east—regions unrivaled in spectacular scenery, local foods, and vacation getaways.

OPPOSITE: Le Clos Saragnat is an apple orchard and *cidrerie* in Cantons-de-l'Est owned by Christian Barthomeuf, who pioneered a unique local product: ice cider.

PREVIOUS PAGES: Hikers in Mont Orford National Park pass a giant boulder. Behind them, at 1,965 feet (599 m), Mont Chauve dominates the horizon, its autumn landscape a vibrant mosaic of reds, oranges, and yellows.

CANTONS-DE-L'EST

BENEDICTINE ABBEY AND STARRY SKIES

Victorian-style architecture, flamboyant autumn landscapes, and an early 20th-century abbey on Lake Memphremagog give the Cantons-de-l'Est (Eastern Townships) their unique cachet. Their vineyards boast world-renowned ciders and trademark ice wines; gastronomic pleasures include cheeses and maple products. The Route des Sommets (Summit Drive) up Mont Mégantic and Mont Ham offers spectacular views—and Mont Mégantic Observatory.

LEFT: Saint Benôit du Lac Abbey overlooks Lake Memphremagog. Gregorian chants of Benedictine monks rise from its walls. The monks, who live in harmony with nature, create local products.

ABOVE: The village of Danville features New England–influenced architecture. The railroad's arrival in the mid-1800s sparked the construction of Victorian-style houses.

ABOVE: Mont Mégantic National Park is renowned for the Vallée des Fantômes, where snowy pines in winter loom like ghosts. At 3,615 feet (1,102 m), the summit of Mont Mégantic offers a dazzling view of a winter paradise for cross-country skiers and snowshoers.

OPPOSITE: Public art shapes the urban landscape of Sherbrooke. Frescoes, sculptures, and commemorative monuments are integral to buildings, parks, and other public places. Artists' talents are in the spotlight, and their creations speak to a rich cultural heritage.

FOLLOWING PAGES: A tour along the roads of Compton Township immerses travelers in a stunning pastoral landscape. This end of the Coaticook River Valley is famous for its beauty and its horizon: Mont Orford rises to the west, the American Appalachians to the south.

OPPOSITE: In Frelighsburg municipality, about a half mile (1 km) from Vermont, Christian Barthomeuf turns his passion for the local *terroir* into celebrated products. A pioneer of Québec artisanal viticulture, he developed the world's first ice cider in 1989. His cultivation methods are based on observing natural cycles and ecological balance. Apples and cold weather combine to create a brew enchanting to the taste buds.

ABOVE RIGHT: North Hatley's greatest asset is its natural environment. Surrounded by mountains on the northern shore of Lake Massawippi, the village's century-old homes, stunning inns, and lakeside parks add undeniable charm to the inherent beauty.

BELOW RIGHT: Harvest time is in full swing at the vineyards of the Brome-Missisquoi area. It's the perfect time to follow the Wine Route. Along this 87-mile (140 km) route linking 22 wineries—some the oldest in Québec— winemakers demonstrate how their grapes are harvested and prepared. Wine tastings, local products, and guided tours are available, and some vineyards even offer a one-day winemaker experience.

TRAVEL DIARY

I t is 5 a.m. and a glance outside gives me a quick status report … Rumor has it that Mont Sutton will accumulate more than 20 inches (50 cm) of snow in this storm. The drive from Montréal is laborious, the road conditions horrendous—but the photos will be worth the trouble.

Mont Sutton stands apart from other Québec mountains. Its ambience is similar to that of mountains in the Canadian west, where skiing is in everyone's DNA. Though not the highest, it boasts abundant, powdery snow and unrivaled woodland and glade skiing. The smallest snowstorm draws scores of ski enthusiasts. From the chairlift I take in the scope of the storm, the slopes appear covered in whipped cream, with delectable peaks here and there.

Within the first few turns, the skiers let out whoops of joy. Visibility is reduced in the swirling snow. At one point my mouth is so full of snow from laughing that I nearly suffocate. My downhill speed picks up. Overconfidence emboldens this daredevil … and there he goes … rolling, head-over-skis. Landing awkwardly in the deep powder, he may need assistance to get back up.

After a break, Corey Anthony, our group's most experienced skier, proposes we head down Fantaisie—a run said to be sheer paradise for the glade skier. Corey glides effortlessly down the narrow paths, weaving in and out of the trees. Mesmerizing. I am delighted to capture his moves on camera.

Mont Sutton is one of many ski centers in the Eastern Townships. With a vertical drop of only 1,509 feet (460 m), it is far from the highest mountain, but it offers glade skiing that forest skiers will find nowhere else. At the first sign of snow, they hit the slopes.

OPPOSITE: Choinière Reservoir, in Yamaska National Park, is a veritable oasis of blue gold—an escape from urban concrete. The reservoir was designed in the 1970s to regulate the water flow from the Yamaska River. Now this vast water basin and its surroundings are highly valued recreational and tourism sites.

ABOVE RIGHT: The town of Bromont, in the shadow of its namesake mountain and close to many bodies of water, is an attractive destination in every season. In winter, skiers take to the 111 runs, which make up the largest lighted night-skiing region in North America.

BELOW RIGHT: Discovering the world of birds is an experience prized by nature lovers and bird-watchers who visit Yamaska National Park and environs. Trails run throughout the park— and all the Eastern Townships—where birders can see species including chickadees, wood ducks, peregrine falcons, owls, and fishing buzzards in woodland, wetland, and mountain habitats. The numbers can be astonishing, depending on the season.

CENTRE-DU-QUÉBEC

CRANBERRIES, ROSES, AND OTHER DELIGHTS

Centre-du-Québec's (Central Québec) fertile soil supports exceptional gardens and specialized crops, from roses to cranberries. Parks like Mont Arthabaska offer stunning views. Forays include Route des Navigateurs (Navigators' Route) along the St. Lawrence; Antiques Roadways & Byways; Route to Gourmet Delights; and stops at rural villages like Scots-influenced Inverness.

LEFT: As a blushing sun sets on the St. Lawrence River, Laviolette Bridge, which connects the cities of Trois-Rivières and Bécancour, disappears beyond the horizon.

ABOVE AND FOLLOWING PAGES: Regional thematic tours guide visitors to appreciate Centre-du-Québec's rivers, forests, and farms raising crops, poultry, and more. Every spring hundreds of thousands of snow geese flock to Febvre Bay in Lake St. Pierre, a UNESCO biosphere reserve (pages 158–159).

OPPOSITE: Located in the St. Lawrence Lowlands and crisscrossed by several rivers, Centre-du-Québec is rich with fertile ground. The Route to Gourmet Delights sends visitors across the region along country roads. Farms and shops selling local products such as cheeses, apples, and cranberry and maple products will tempt even the pickiest eaters.

ABOVE RIGHT: Market gardening and farming have shaped Centre-du-Québec. Rich orchards, cranberry fields, and canola fields bring color to the landscape of this region. Local artisans are eager to introduce visitors to their fruit and vegetable harvests—like this variety of radishes—fresh every day.

BELOW RIGHT: The millers of this region produce a wide variety of high-quality organic flours, and bakers are proud to offer an abundance of delicious breads made with these stone-ground flours. Great bread is a farm-to-table art; enjoying it right out of the oven at a Centre-du-Québec bakery is simply divine.

MONTÉRÉGIE

300-YEAR CULTURAL LANDSCAPE

Montérégie's French- and British-built towns and First Nations communities help tell its 300-year story, with destinations such as the Droulers-Tsiionhiakwatha Archaeological Site and Chambly Canal. Home to Canada's largest hot-air balloon festival, this region also boasts two national parks and thematic routes like the Route des Cidres (Cider Route) that invite adventure, beauty, and gustatory pleasures.

LEFT: Îles de Boucherville National Park, an oasis in an urban landscape, is known for its bike trails and kayak routes.

ABOVE AND FOLLOWING PAGES: The 1906 lighthouse on Île du Moine, one of the Îles de Sorel, is powered by a solar panel. Mont Saint-Bruno National Park (pages 164 and 165), a hidden jewel near Montréal, features an arch bridge, an early structure.

LEFT: Fort Lennox, located on Île aux Noix on the Richelieu River, was a 19th-century defense point for the British. Visitors can explore the buildings and garrison life, and try out two red Adirondack chairs, a signature of Parks Canada placed throughout national parks. Try spotting them here.

ABOVE: A surfer hits the rapids on the Richelieu River. Parallel to it, the quieter Chambly Canal, a national historic site, stretches 12 miles (19.5 km) with nine locks. Once used for transporting wood to the United States, the canal now welcomes pleasure boats.

OPPOSITE: Young or old, everyone loves a little sweetness when maple syrup starts to flow in the spring. Montérégie is a popular destination to enjoy maple products in all their forms. Traditional sugar shacks serve a variety of maple-based seasonal cuisines. *Oreilles de crisse* (deep-fried smoked pork jowls topped with maple syrup), maple ham, *grands-pères dans le sirop* (sweetened, boiled cake balls), sugar pie, and maple syrup crepes are bound to satisfy even the most demanding sweet tooths.

RIGHT: Maple taffy on snow is a Québec delight, mostly consumed at sugaring-off parties from mid-March to the end of April: Groups gather to tap sap from maple trees and then boil and thicken it into syrup to make varied sweets. This treat started as a staple for indigenous peoples, who called the maple sap "sweet water" and survived through the late winter months on products made from it. Today, Québec produces two-thirds of the world's maple syrup, a product that has become a symbol of Quebecois identity.

GREATER MONTRÉAL

CITY PULSING WITH LIFE

Montréal amazes, resonates, lights up. To live the Montréal experience is to uncover a banquet of festivals, concerts, museums, and restaurants. With multicultural neighborhoods that proudly perpetuate their traditions, Montréal is best discovered on foot. Pedestrian streets open in warm months pulsate with life. In the cold, a 20-mile-long (32 km) network of underground tunnels called the RÉSO provides access to downtown venues.

LEFT: Restaurants on Boulevard Saint-Laurent, called the Main; rue Saint-Denis; rue Sainte-Catherine; and in Plateau Mont-Royal invite visitors to absorb Montréal's spirit.

ABOVE AND FOLLOWING PAGES: Historic Notre Dame de Bon Secours Chapel on celebrated rue Saint-Paul dates from 1771 and features a museum and archaeological site from 1675. Viewed from the quays of the Old Port across the St. Lawrence River, Montréal lights up at dusk (pages 172–173).

ABOVE: With its remarkable religious heritage, Montréal's Notre Dame Basilica offers a wealth of historic treasures. Across the vaulted ceiling, art and symbolism against a deep blue background evoke "the way to heavenly bliss." Staring into the intense blue, visitors are fascinated by this mystical composition and its name. .

OPPOSITE: Rue Saint-Paul, Montréal's oldest street, is elegant in the winter's blue hour. At the heart of Old Montréal, century-old buildings, art galleries, Place Jacques-Cartier, Marché Bonsecours, and Old Port can all be explored.

FOLLOWING PAGES: An autumn morning (page 176) in Plateau Mont-Royal shows off the neighborhood's unique character: green spaces with shops, cultural sites, and recreation facilities. Antonio Park (page 177), a Korean-Argentine-Quebecois, named best Canadian chef in 2015 by the Terroir Symposium, draws inspiration from his cultural background—as do many Montréal chefs.

OPPOSITE: The window of Joseph Ponton Costumes is an inviting entrée to the shop inside: one of the oldest costume stores in Québec, established in 1865. Joseph Ponton, a barber and haberdasher, began the business after acquiring costumes from a theater troupe. Today, the shop carries more than 15,000 costumes, each waiting to be brought to life.

ABOVE RIGHT: Architecture reflecting the city's French heritage looms above Place d'Armes, the main square in the heart of Old Montréal. Here stands the monument to Maisonneuve, one of the city's founders. The square's atmosphere is both historic and contemporary, thanks to the more than five million people who cross it every year on the way to work or to discover Old Montréal's hidden charms.

BELOW RIGHT: The Kondiaronk Lookout from Mont Royal city park offers the best views of Montréal and its surrounding landscape. Here the subtleties of morning light in autumn veil the waking city. On the hill above Montréal proper, Mont Royal encompasses 470 acres (190 ha), a veritable green oasis and favorite spot for nature lovers and fitness buffs. An illuminated cross at its summit can be seen from 50 miles (80 km) away, and has been a part of the Montréal skyline since 1924.

"MONTRÉAL WAS BUILT ON A DREAM, ON AN IDEAL OF HARMONY AND ACCORD AMONG ALL PEOPLES ... MONTRÉAL IS A CITY WHERE PEOPLE CAN LIVE TOGETHER AND CELEBRATE THEIR DIVERSITY. LOVE MONTRÉAL FOR ITS ARCHITECTURE, FOR ITS NEIGHBORHOODS, AND FOR ITS CUISINE, BUT ABOVE ALL, LOVE IT FOR ITS INHABITANTS.
VIVE MONTRÉAL!"

—DENIS CODERRE, MAYOR OF MONTRÉAL

The Montréal Botanical Garden, one of the world's largest, holds grand events throughout the year. In autumn, the Gardens of Light festival re-creates an ancient Chinese village using silk lanterns in shapes from people to dragons.

LANAUDIÈRE
VIBRANT OFFERINGS

This region's rich natural surroundings include part of the ancient Laurentian Mountains. Quaint accommodations of French, British, Irish, and Scottish influence; heritage routes; and gastronomic experiences showcasing local products from lamb to bison, from honey to squash, are among Lanaudière's vibrant offerings. Each July an outdoor amphitheater hosts Canada's prestigious classical music event, Le Festival de Lanaudière. Summer theater, art galleries, and historic buildings such as the 18th-century Île des Moulins, reward culture enthusiasts, as do the arts, song, and dance of the Atikamekw people in the First Nations village of Manawan.

LEFT: Mont Garceau in Saint-Donat is Lanaudière's highest mountain, and its ski center is a family favorite. These snowy revelers are testament to the Quebecois' love for winter.

ABOVE: The lakes and rivers in the Pimbina sector of Mont Tremblant National Park make it a paddling paradise.

OPPOSITE: The Cuthbert Chapel, today a historic monument, was the first Protestant church erected in Québec. Modest and light-filled, this small chapel in Berthierville tells the story of James Cuthbert, who became the first English seigneur here in 1765. In modern times, the chapel is a tourist site and exhibition venue. Unusually, its bell tower is located at one side, instead of in the building's center.

RIGHT: Crossing the Lanaudière countryside is an opportunity to explore a region of 58 square miles (150 sq km), boasting incredible diversity. Travel through towns and villages bustling with activities and festivals. Follow the river and discover wide-open spaces and holiday destinations. Meet friendly people, relax in an outdoor café, and promise yourself to come back soon.

FOLLOWING PAGES: This rich area has earned the name Terrebonne, or "good land." The lively city of Old Terrebonne, which hides a historic neighborhood along the banks of the Mille Îles River, is a center of culture and history for the area.

LEFT: Lanaudière's mountainous landscape is split with rocky faults where rivers run and waterfalls crash. Footpaths bordering the waters allow visitors breathtaking views.

ABOVE: Agritourism tours take visitors through the highlights of local agriculture. Horses, bison, and goats are raised at properties along the tour route. One place, Arpents Roses Farm, raises only pigs.

LAURENTIDES

NATURE AT ITS BEST

At the heart of the Laurentian Mountains, this region is endowed with exceptional natural attributes, thanks to its diverse ecosystems. Pristine valleys and rushing rivers send invitations to hit the slopes, paddle the currents, or discover superb resorts and golf courses. Discover breathtaking Mont Tremblant National Park and unique P'tit Train du Nord linear park—a bike path built over an old railway line for year-round cycling, skating, cross-country skiing, or snowmobiling. Thematic routes, such as the Chemin du Terroir (Path of Cultivation), feature beekeeping, alpaca breeding, and more.

LEFT: The Hautes-Laurentides—the Laurentides' northern area—is an agritourist region nestled in rich, green wilderness. Enjoy a country dinner in Ferme-Neuve with Devil's Mountain as backdrop.

ABOVE: An aerial shot at sunset reveals the Laurentides' mountainous terrain under a blanket of fog. Hills, mountains, lakes, and rivers make up most of this enormous region of 8,494 square miles (22,000 sq km).

The crystal clear water of Lake of Two Mountains stretches 4.3 miles (7 km) along its beach, part of the splendid natural richness of Oka National Park. Hikers can follow trails to the Calvaire d'Oka, a historic complex of three chapels and four oratories dating to the early 1740s. Views from the Calvaire d'Oka trailhead reveal the lake and the Adirondack Mountains.

Mont Tremblant sits at the heart of a stunning environment crisscrossed by rivers and dotted with green oases. A skier's favorite destination, the mountain and pedestrian village at its base pulse to the seasons. In winter, in the last golden light of day, an après-ski ambience settles into the village. In summer, the vibrant atmosphere continues, as hikers descend from mountain trails to enjoy outdoor restaurants and music.

OPPOSITE: The rivière du Diable, or Devil's River, some 51 miles (82 km) long, is named for its tumultuous nature—its rapids, waterfalls, eddies, and bends, which in the past challenged log drivers as they navigated the waters, and sometimes claimed lives. The Devil's River also offers easy stretches and quiet moments for contemplation. Here canoeists drift through the fog of a warm morning on still water.

RIGHT: The luxurious mixed forest and sandy bends of the Devil's River complete this panorama of the Laurentian Mountains. Located in Mont Tremblant National Park, this labyrinth of valleys and hills sits at 984 to 1,312 feet (300–400 m) high, while Mont Tremblant towers over them at 3,175 feet (968 m). The magic of the Laurentians and their ever changing beauty charms visitors at any time of the year.

LEFT: These beehives, located in the countryside of the Hautes-Laurentides, represent Anicet Desrochers and Anne-Virginie Schmidt's true passion: bee guardianship and breeding.

ABOVE: During Québec's short summers, the fields are rich with flowers of all kinds. Local honey comes in a variety of colors, flavors, and textures, influenced by the nectar of the flowers the bees visit.

THE QUÉBEC TRAVELER

PLANNING GUIDE FOR CENTRAL QUÉBEC

1-DAY ADVENTURE: CANTONS-DE-L'EST | The Chemin des Cantons, or Townships Trail, is a well-marked tourism route through the rolling hills, farms, and forests of the Eastern Townships. It takes visitors through 31 picturesque towns and highlights 27 attractions related to the region's Anglo-American heritage, including museums, parks, and historic homes. Focus on one or two regions, or spend the day driving from one end of the route to the other, a distance of 267 miles (430 km). Maps and other information are available in tourist information offices and online.

2-DAY ADVENTURE: LAURENTIDES | Located just an hour north of Montréal, the Laurentides region is a year-round playground. Devote your first day to exploring Oka National Park. Rent a fat bike, whose oversize tires are ideal for traversing snow and sand, or take a pedal boat out on the water. The magnificent Calvaire d'Oka trail is an easy 2.7-mile (4.4 km) round-trip hike that leads to a panoramic view marked by three white chapels erected in 1740–42. Four small chapels called oratories line the route. Spend the second day at the mountain resort of Mont Tremblant, where seasonal activities include golf, skiing, dogsledding, ice fishing, dune buggy tours, horseback riding, and more. Enjoy a casual meal with a view at the summit or head down to the pedestrian village, where restaurants, bars, and cafés mix with boutique shops, souvenir stores, and two art galleries.

3-DAY ADVENTURE: GREATER MONTRÉAL | Begin with a walking tour of Old Montréal. Historic buildings line the Place d'Armes public square, including Notre Dame Basilica, erected in the 19th century, as well as Saint Sulpice Seminary, begun in 1684. Window-shop along rue Saint-Paul, and spend time in the nearby science or history museum. Enjoy dinner at Marché Bonsecours, the city's oldest and largest public market. On day two get a taste of Montréal's diversity, and its culinary array, in Plateau Mont-Royal. Stick to boulevard Saint-Laurent, called the Main, or navigate the neighborhood's grid of streets. After a meal at one of the area's delis, French bistros, or bagel shops, head to Parc des Amériques or St. Jean Baptiste Church for an evening concert. Spend the final day at Space for Life, the city's complex of four natural science museums, including the Botanical Garden and its famous Insectarium, the Biodôme with its four distinct ecosystems, and two immersion theaters at the Rio Tinto Alcan Planetarium.

Located in the heart of Montréal, the Palais des congrès de Montréal convention center is distinguished by its international renown and unique modern architecture.

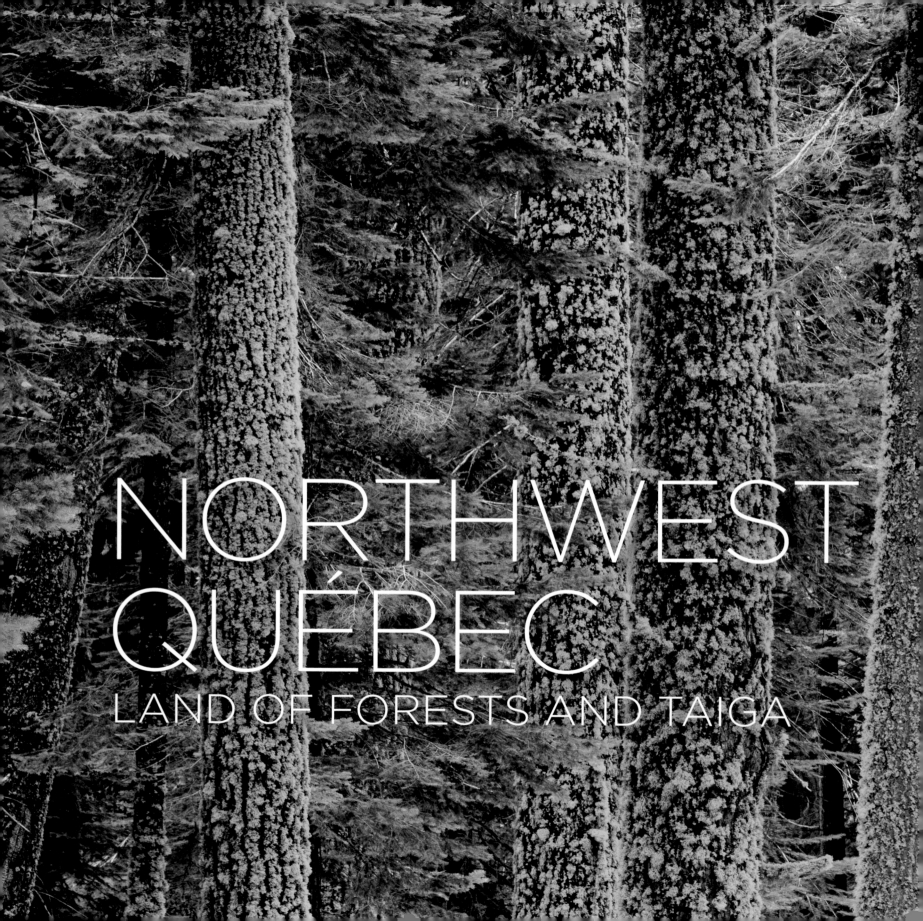

NORTHWEST QUÉBEC

LAND OF FORESTS AND TAIGA

SINUOUS AND SWIFT, the legendary Ottawa River has shaped life and landscape in Northwest Québec for centuries. From its mouth, where it empties into the St. Lawrence River, early explorers paddled west against the current, through today's Outaouais (Ottawa) region. In the 18th century the river carried fleets of fur-trading voyageurs in canoes through northwest Québec and west toward the Great Lakes. Later a venue for log drivers of the timber trade, today the river is harnessed for hydroelectric power. It also forms the natural boundary between two provinces and cultures: Anglophone Ontario to the south and Francophone Québec to the north.

Heading northwest from Outaouais, the Ottawa runs through a rift valley cradling Lake Timiskaming, in today's Abitibi-Témiscamingue region. This region's unique character combines Témiscamingue's Laurentian forest, farmlands, and temperate climate and Abitibi's metal-enriched soil and boreal forest. Here, in the Laurentian Mountains, lies the Ottawa's source. From nearby Aiguebelle National Park, which straddles the divide between two watersheds, the Ottawa flows south to the St. Lawrence while the Harricana and other rivers flow north to James and Hudson Bays.

Running north from Aiguebelle, these rivers pass through the Eeyou Istchee Baie-James region, home to communities of Cree and Inuit. To visit here is to encounter raw and arid nature, and a captivating people proud of their land.

OPPOSITE: The art of constructing snowshoes has remained intact in Oujé-Bougoumou, a Cree community in the Eeyou Istchee Baie-James region. Members have maintained a powerful connection to their ancestral lifestyle. Their deep respect for tradition is passed down from generation to generation.

PREVIOUS PAGES: In the forested valley of the Dumoine River, this rich vegetation is watered by the constant spray from a roaring waterfall, which imparts a luxuriant sheen.

OUTAOUAIS

RICH HERITAGE AND SPECTACULAR SCENERY

With its southern border shaped by the Ottawa (Outaouais) River, the region of Outaouais thrives on its location. Along the river, some 373 miles (600 km) of biking and walking paths connect gardens, parks, and museums. The Canadian Museum of History, in Gatineau, showcases more than a million artifacts and a First Peoples Hall; and Gatineau Park features spectacular scenery and activities for outdoor enthusiasts. Beyond the riverbanks, Outaouais lakes, forests, and farmlands delight visitors. The regional farm-tourism route seduces the palate with mouthwatering food stops.

LEFT: Built in 1898 and designated a historic monument in 2006, the Félix-Gabriel Marchand Bridge in Fort-Coulonge is one of Québec's treasures.

ABOVE AND FOLLOWING PAGES: The Canadian Museum of History in Gatineau was designed by renowned Aboriginal architect Douglas Cardinal. The Zizanie-des-Marais trail in Plaisance National Park (page 206) features a floating boardwalk. Brylee Farm (page 207) is an innovative grass farm.

OPPOSITE: The Lièvre River is one of the main tributaries of the Ottawa River, flowing south for some 200 miles (322 km). Throughout its journey the river traverses numerous lakes and runs through a large valley where it bends and turns, sometimes sandwiched between mountains. The region is ideal for those seeking a rural experience with rich scenery.

RIGHT: The bike paths of Plaisance National Park cover some 18.5 miles (30 km) across islands and peninsulas at the heart of the Ottawa River. This enchanting natural oasis is inhabited by more than 250 species of birds, numerous small mammals, and turtles. As the park's name suggests, a visit is a pleasurable experience—a discovery of vibrant nature shaped by diverse habitats, from forests to wetlands.

FOLLOWING PAGES: Gatineau provides a magnificent view of Parliament Hill, which lies on the Ontario side of the Ottawa River. While Gatineau is the principal urban center of the Outaouais region, its geographic location imparts the dual advantages of urban living and the great outdoors. The city lies in close proximity to popular parks and other natural sites. Gatineau Park, for instance, some 15 minutes from the city center, offers a multitude of outdoor sports and nautical activities year-round.

ABITIBI-TÉMISCAMINGUE

ENCHANTING PEOPLE AND TREASURES

Majestic nature and generous, multitalented people are the jewels of Abitibi-Témiscamingue. Renowned for its wildlife, the region boasts historic and recent treasures: Fort Témiscamingue, a 17th-century fur trading post, Roman-Byzantine–style St. Teresa of Avila Cathedral in Amos, and the Museum of Art, the region's first, in Rouyn-Noranda.

LEFT: In Abitibi-Ouest, the Antoine wetland is a wildlife and plant observation site on the shores of Lake Abitibi. Walkways and belvederes give access to magnificent nature.

ABOVE: Ville-Marie was anointed the "most beautiful village in Québec" in 2012. Century-old Victorian-style homes bordering Lake Timiskaming shape the landscape of this little corner of paradise.

OPPOSITE: Fog rises slowly over the wetlands around the Premier Lac du Portage du Sauvage, a lake whose name refers to the wildlands across which paddlers carry their canoes. Not far away, the rapids of the Kipawa River can be heard. Bordered by white and red pines, the river flows some 11 miles (18 km) toward Lake Timiskaming. The scenery is breathtaking, but only paddlers experienced at navigating its many rapids ever see—and appreciate—its beauty.

ABOVE RIGHT: A twinkle in his eye, pilot Claude Barrette grins after three heady hours of freedom in the clouds. The seaplane is part and parcel of the lifestyle in regions where lakes and rivers abound.

BELOW RIGHT: Imposing attractions grace Opemican National Park: Lake Kipawa, a labyrinth of large bays and hundreds of islands; Lake Timiskaming, 67 miles (108 km) in length and surrounded by steep cliffs up to 229 feet (70 m) high; Pointe Opémican, with its historic Aboriginal and logging site; and the Kipawa River with its rapids and spectacular 88.5-foot (27 m) waterfalls, stacked one on top of the other. This unique park has the right to boast of its position on the face of Canada's $10 bill.

LEFT: In Duhamel-Ouest, near Ville-Marie, time seems to pass at an altogether different pace as evening falls. The small rural road that leads straight to Île-du-Collège fosters a sense of tranquility and a lifestyle in harmony with this agricultural milieu.

ABOVE: Located in La Vallée-de-l'Or, mining town Malartic's streets still feature boomtown-style buildings from the early 1900s; nearby is Canada's largest open-pit gold mine.

"CRADLE OF MY INFANCY, LAND OF MY HERITAGE, SOURCE OF MY INSPIRATION. ABITIBI-TÉMISCAMINGUE, YOU HAVE NOURISHED MY HEART, MY DREAMS, AND MY PASSIONS. YOU HAVE FINE-TUNED MY SENSITIVITY TO THE NUANCES OF THE SKY WITH ITS EXCEPTIONAL ILLUMINATION, AND YOU HAVE GUIDED ME TO NEW HORIZONS."

—MATHIEU DUPUIS

LEFT: Near the border with Ontario, Mont Chaudron is a true geologic anomaly: An inselberg, or isolated small mountain, it rises abruptly from a virtually level plain. The 1,729-foot (527 m) mountain is named for the upside-down cauldron—or *chaudron*—it resembles. Its unique perspective is magnified during the blue hour.

FOLLOWING PAGES: A true guardian of the Kékéko Hills, Marc-André Dupuis (page 220) knows these mountains. Since childhood he has walked, climbed, canoed, and admired them through each season. Not far from the town of Rouyn-Noranda and rich with geologic history, they beckon to those who long to be in nature. The shores of Lake Renaud—near Arntfield, a neighborhood of Rouyn-Noranda—boast magnificent lookouts for sunset viewing (page 221). This area's exceptional natural attractions include the Kékéko Hills, Mont Chaudron, Mont Kanasuta, and numerous lakes abundant with fish.

OPPOSITE: At day's end, the ambience of Lake Chassignol provides a moment of escape. This body of water is juxtaposed with Lake Preissac, which plunges into the Kinojévis River, a tributary of the Ottawa River. Exploration of this area reveals a lookout tower with a breathtaking view; a path past a venerated boulder, called the "walkway of the millennial rock"; and year-round fishing.

ABOVE RIGHT: At the venerable age of 89, seasoned canoer Germain Allen paddles on and portages through the waterways of his favorite Lake Buies. Canyons, craggy bends, rock-encircled whirlpools, spongy moss: Such a magnificent setting is ample reward for the long distance paddled.

BELOW RIGHT: The Abijévis Hills in Aiguebelle National Park shimmer beneath their autumn coat. Within the hills, Lake La Haie is connected to two cliffs by a 72-foot-high (22 m) suspended walkway with its own "legend." Created by aspiring writers, it begins: "On this territory we now tread, there were once giants." The saga of a courageous patriarch giant ensues, until "battle weary, the giant gave in and crouched down."

FOLLOWING PAGES: The quality of cultural events in Rouyn-Noranda shines beyond the town's borders. The Abitibi-Témiscamingue Film Festival in Rouyn-Noranda has been credentialed since 1982. In summer Vieux-Noranda and the banks of Osisko Lake host renowned artistic events and welcome thousands of enthusiasts. From the World Guitar Festival to theater productions, from music and fireworks displays to the popular music gathering Festival de Musique Émergente, life in Rouyn-Noranda moves to the rhythm of the arts.

OPPOSITE: Springtime gently liberates the waters of Lake Abitibi near L'Île Nepawa. Located in Abitibi-Ouest, this shallow lake played an early role in the expansion of the fur trade and, later, in the development of the region's lumber industry. Today, Abitibi-Ouest counts 21 economic hubs, including La Sarre, the most populous town.

RIGHT: On the banks of the Harricana River, the town of Amos glows sublimely at the blue hour. Once a fur trading outpost, Amos was Abitibi's first settlement, in the early 1900s. Its largely French heritage is reflected in this imposing Roman-Byzantine–style cathedral. The spring water that flows along its glacier-formed ridges is deemed one of the world's best.

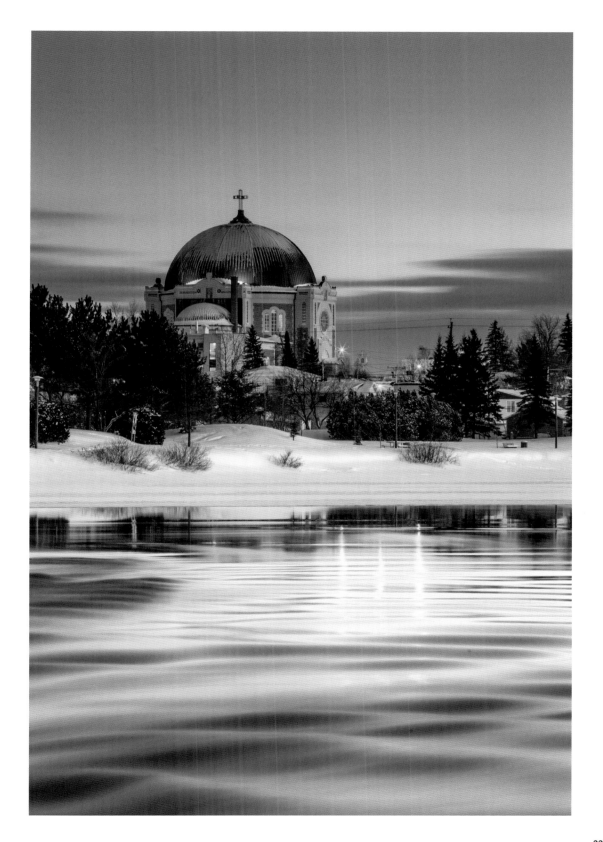

EEYOU ISTCHEE BAIE-JAMES
REGION OF TRADITIONS AND MODERNITY

This region covers slightly more than one-fifth of Québec. Along its northernmost rivers and lakes thrive nine communities of the Cree First Nation of Eeyou Istchee—meaning "the people's land." Despite mining installations and hydroelectric dams, nature and rigorous climate remain masters of the area, as evidenced in magnificent boreal dawns against the endless horizon. The residents maintain a fierce "nordicity"—a uniquely northern Canadian approach to living.

LEFT: In bitter January cold, sunlight sparkling through the icy fog above Rainbow Rapid allows it to live up to its name. In the area of Chibougamau, one of the principal towns of Eeyou Istchee Baie-James, grand nature rules.

ABOVE: Dressed in traditional Cree garb of rabbit pelts, a young boy on a hunting trip with his father will learn the art of setting a snare.

229

OPPOSITE: Not far from the Cree community of Waskaganish, the Smokey Hill Rapid on the Rupert River is a cultural meeting ground incomparable for its beauty and seclusion. For members of the Cree community and their guests, an evening spent in a tepee by the rapid, hearing its deafening roar, is transport to a world beyond the imagination.

ABOVE RIGHT: Along the paths of Obalski Regional Park, hikers will encounter a forest mosaic that changes at every turn. Delectable small fruit, spongy mosses: Nature's smells stirred up by the slightest breeze entice the senses.

BELOW RIGHT: This bountiful harvest of lobster mushrooms took place in the woods not far from the Cree community of Oujé-Bougoumou. The lobster mushroom, actually a fungus that grows on some kinds of mushrooms, turns orange-red and has a seafoodlike flavor.

FOLLOWING PAGES: In a fascinating chance encounter on the banks of the Rupert River, professional hunting guide Ken Taylor (page 232) gives visitors insight into the winter forests and fauna before revealing his passion: traditional bow hunting. It turns out that he is a living legend in the area. After a fishing session at the mouth of the Rupert River, on Lake Mistassini, a shore lunch is rapidly prepared from the morning's bounty (page 233). On the menu: walleye with onions, and potatoes.

OPPOSITE: After a gray start to the day, the northern sun brightens a shoal of the Vieux Comptoir River not far from the village of Wemindji. Aquatic plants and trees bring harmonious texture to the landscape.

ABOVE RIGHT: Cree master trapper Angus Mayappo steers his long, motor-powered freighter canoe along the sinuous Opinaca River leading to his hunting camp in the heart of the taiga, where he shares Cree traditions—from raising a tepee to cooking Cree meals—with travelers.

BELOW RIGHT: Bannock, the traditional wheat flatbread of First Nations peoples, is made with the basic ingredients of wheat, lard, salt, and water. Recipes are as numerous and varied as the families who create them. In Cree tradition, bannock is cooked over a wood fire inside the tepee.

TRAVEL DIARY

CREE ANCESTRAL GROUNDS

We take advantage of the good weather to go canoeing along the Vieux Comptoir River that flows into James Bay. As we return from our outing, after a pause for a lunch on shore, we come upon the ancient Cree community of Wemindji bathed in golden light. Now moved 28 miles (45 km) north to the mouth of the Maquatua River, the modern community's residents still visit this ancient ground. The echo of tribal chants from a powwow float across the river to our ears. We are wide-eyed and speechless. It is as if we've traveled back in time. A single moment of genuine adventure sends shivers up our spine with every stroke of the paddle. These moments of rare authenticity nearly erase from memory the thousands of miles traveled on isolated roads. The journey has not always been a pleasure outing: The ever present threat of a mechanical failure or other event in these larger-than-life regions hovers perpetually at the back of one's mind. But for those daring to brave the north, the adventure will remain unforgettable.

An event of meeting and cultural exchange, the powwow is rich in color. In this extraordinary visual and aural experience, traditional garb bears witness to First Nations' individual identities. Within each community, such as the Cree pictured here, the songs and dances of powwows evolve with every generation.

LEFT: Bush pilots of the north swear by the legendary de Havilland Beaver bush plane. Docked for the night, this one will take its passengers beyond the point where the remote Trans-Taiga Road ends.

ABOVE: Under a brilliant Milky Way, dozens of freighter canoes line the long rocky beach near Chisasibi, a village on the south bank of La Grande River, Québec's third longest river after the St. Lawrence and Ottawa.

THE QUÉBEC TRAVELER

1 DAY ADVENTURE: OUTAOUAIS | Situated just across the river from Ottawa, the nation's capital, Gatineau offers all the amenities of a large city with none of the stress and congestion. Spend the morning at the popular Canadian Museum of History, and then rent a bicycle and take to one of the themed bike pathways that snake through the city. The city's annual hot-air balloon festival takes place in early September.

2-DAY ADVENTURE: ABITIBI-TÉMISCAMINGUE | Start by learning about this region's rich natural resources in the small city of Val-d'Or ("valley of gold"). Prospectors discovered gold here in 1923, and the Canadian Malartic Mine just outside the city—the nation's largest operating open-pit gold mine—offers tours. Become a miner for the day at Cité de l'Or, where visitors can tour a former underground mine as well as the aboveground village that supported it. The Mineralogical Museum in Malartic showcases regional geology. Spend day two exploring the area's other natural wonders in Aiguebelle National Park, located about 31 miles (50 km) north of Rouyn-Noranda, another city shaped by Canada's mining history. Travel billions of years back in time on the 1.9-mile (3 km) La Traverse, a loop, which includes a 72-foot (22 m) suspension bridge across a geologic fault.

3-DAY ADVENTURE: EEYOU ISTCHEE BAIE-JAMES | Located 435 miles (700 km) north of Montréal, the Eeyou Istchee Baie-James region promises vast expanses of quiet wilderness rich with Cree history. On day one explore the city of Chibougamau, known for its outdoor recreation opportunities as well as the small but unique Quasar Planetarium. On day two leave Chibougamau for Oujé-Bougoumou, a small Cree village on the shore of Lake Opemisca. Here visitors experience traditional culture and cuisine alongside the community's residents. On day three make the 207-mile (333 km) drive from Chibougamau to Matagami, start of the Route de la Baie-James. Bumpy in spots, this road stretches north 388 miles (620 km) through remote boreal forest to the town of Radisson. There is only one gas station (km 381), and no other services, along the route, so fill up with gas before heading out and ensure your vehicle is in good working order. Stop for the night at one of the campgrounds that line the route at regular intervals or continue on to Radisson.

Snowmobile riding remains one of the most popular activities in the untouched expanses of the Eeyou Istchee Baie-James region. When conditions are perfect, rider and machine operate as one in the powder.

FAR NORTH QUÉBEC
WHERE GIANTS WALK

ACCESSIBLE ONLY BY AIR, Far North Québec promises an exceptional adventure on Quebecois soil. With its single region of Nunavik spreading across 196,000 square miles (507,600 sq km), this area north of the 55th parallel is larger than the U.S. state of California and includes both Arctic and subarctic climate zones. Immensity, challenging climate, diverse ecosystems: Here the meaning of the "law of nature" is fully realized. The absence of trees transforms the landscape into one gigantic thoroughfare, and the sky disappears into an endless horizon.

Larger than life, Nunavik seems to have been created expressly for those of incredible strength: its people, polar bears, whales, musk oxen, arctic wolves. It is also a land of great migrations. Caribou may roam 1,864 miles (3,000 km) during their annual migration.

Numbering some 10,750, the resident Inuit, who call themselves Nunavimmiut, inhabit Hudson Bay to the west, and Hudson Strait and Ungava Bay to the north. Generous and welcoming, they are quick to put at ease newcomers unsettled by the Arctic's stark grandeur. For more than 4,000 years the Inuit have learned the Arctic's deepest secrets of survival. Despite the comforts of contemporary living, time-honored skills endure. To watch an Inuit build an igloo, the ancestral shelter, is awe-inspiring—among the wonders of the people and creatures, the vast spaces, and the reigning silence of this place.

OPPOSITE: Beneath soothing lights of the aurora borealis, St. James Church of Salluit dominates a frozen winter landscape.

PREVIOUS PAGES: Adamie Kulula of Quaqtaq village never goes seal hunting without his traditional caribou-skin anorak. A genuine tool of survival, its sturdiness and warmth guard against unexpected blizzards in the Nunavik winters.

NUNAVIK
LIVING IN SYNC WITH NATURE

The region's nordicity—its uniquely northern Canadian approach to living—and the warmth of its people imbue Nunavik with its unique character. Heirs of ancestral knowledge, the Inuit, or Nunavimmiut, live in harmony with the taiga, Arctic tundra, pack ice, lakes, and rivers. The people are proud of their heritage and honor it through stone sculptures and engravings that depict their way of life. The polar bear, today a symbol of the Arctic whose survival is threatened by the melting sea ice, is a recurring figure. Exploring Nunavik brings appreciation of a world of incomparable beauty—as grand as it is different.

LEFT: Pools of water dotting the tundra ice are a source of high-quality drinking water for the Inuit. As they cross the crystal clear ice, some Inuit say they see arctic char swimming beneath their feet.

ABOVE: A stacked-stone figure called an *inunnguaq*—meaning "like a human"—reigns over an Arctic desert plateau. Integral to Inuit culture, these *inunnguat*, sometimes called *inuksuit*, often mark sacred places or hunting spots.

OPPOSITE: Kangiqsujuaq, meaning "the large bay" in Inuktitut, is also known as Wakeham Bay, after an English sea captain who explored nearby Hudson Bay in 1897. One of the most beautiful Inuit villages in Nunavik, Kangiqsujuaq lies in a valley covered in luxuriant vegetation and surrounded by spectacular mountains. Within the village, frescoes brighten the buildings. Kangiqsujuaq is located about 6 miles (10 km) from the Hudson Strait, which links the Atlantic Ocean and Hudson Bay. Not far from the village is an archaeological site harboring petroglyphs carved some 1,200 years ago.

ABOVE RIGHT: Ungava Bay is among the world's best places to observe icebergs. At Kangiqsujuaq an iceberg has chosen to winter in the middle of Ungava Bay—for the viewing pleasure of the community's 600-plus residents.

BELOW RIGHT: Berthe A. Kulula contemplates the tundra during a walk around Quaqtaq on Ungava Bay. She proudly wears her *amautik*, a traditional Inuit outer garment with a large pouch beneath the hood, designed for carrying infants and keeping them warm.

"I'VE REALLY TRIED TO LIVE SOMEWHERE FARTHER SOUTH, BUT I ALWAYS RETURNED TO THE SOURCE. WHAT I LOVE MORE THAN ANYTHING IN THE WORLD IS THAT HERE, IN MY 'FREE COUNTRY,' WE CAN GAZE FAR, VERY FAR INTO THE DISTANCE."

—ADAMIE KULULA, INUIT GUIDE

LEFT: With my guide, Adamie Kulula, I watch the sun set over Ungava Bay. He tells me about his lifestyle, his dreams. "Here," he says, "tranquility reigns. When the wind dies, one can feel the sun's warmth." It is spring, and the bay frees itself slowly from the ice. We glimpse beluga whales surfacing for air beneath golden geysers in the last ray of light.

FOLLOWING PAGES: As fall comes to the tundra at the 62nd parallel, a group of Inuit fisherman set up their camp against the vast landscape. At the far end of Lake François-Malherbe, an isolated downpour heralds the rigors of winter and the snow that covers this corner of the world nine months of the year.

OPPOSITE: Caribou, kings of the tundra, migrate according to a regular cycle. In spring immense herds gather and begin to move north toward calving grounds. The females, followed by their young, lead the way, and the males close the ranks, falling farther and farther behind as the herds advance. The caribou may roam nearly 1,864 miles (3,000 km) during this journey. In summer the herds continue to move, feeding on grasses, leaves, and flowers. Toward the end of August the return migration begins, and the caribou move south along the same paths—giving hunters an advantage.

ABOVE RIGHT: The Déception River flows along the southwest shore of Déception Bay, and past the village of Déception, before pouring into the Hudson Strait.

BELOW RIGHT: Majestic snow geese measure up to three feet (91.5 cm) in length. From their winter nesting grounds in the United States they return to the Canadian tundra for nesting season. Their arrival to and departure from the Far North are tied to the warm-weather availability of food such as plants and invertebrates.

FOLLOWING PAGES: One of Québec's northernmost Inuit villages, Salluit means "the thin ones" in Inuktitut (pages 256–257). Legend holds that their ancestors nearly starved because of scarce wildlife. Peter Boy Ittukallak of Puvirnituq, at left (pages 258–259), a master ice sculptor, holds the record for building the world's largest igloo. He practices his craft at right.

TRAVEL DIARY

Salluit is one of the northernmost Inuit villages in Québec. Airborne, I view the immensity of this untamed territory as it passes under the wings of our bush plane, a DHC-6 Twin Otter. Turning to his passengers, the young captain is fervent: "I wish you a great flight in the best of Canadian aircraft." We land, and as I open the door to the plane, the temperature is a gripping minus 31°F (-35°C). On the snow-encrusted tarmac, the crunch beneath my boots—designed to withstand temperatures of minus 148°F (-100°C)—makes me smile. This crackling of hardened snow truly evokes the Far North!

When I arrive at the village center, I realize that the best vantage point for pursuing the aurora borealis is in the mountains to the northeast. I inquire about polar bears ... and I am told reassuringly: "There is no alert at this time." But there is no guarantee that I won't have a serendipitous encounter. I scale the mountain by the light of my headlamp and arrive at the top in time for the grand spectacle's first display. Upon seeing the sumptuous curtains of colored light dancing under the starry canopy, it is difficult to remain standing. The feeling is so intense that I almost forget about polar bears ... almost.

LEFT: Swirling northern lights illuminate the sky above the mountains around the village of Salluit. The sense of isolation in this vast and arid arctic desert quickly dissipates with the stunning display.

FOLLOWING PAGES: Robust and always ready to work, sled dogs play an important role in the traditional Nunavik lifestyle. The relationship with the *qimmit*— Inuktitut for "dog"—has proved essential to survival.

THE QUÉBEC TRAVELER

PLANNING GUIDE FOR FAR NORTH QUÉBEC

1-DAY ADVENTURE | Accessible only by air, the village of Quaqtaq lies more than 1,300 miles (2,100 km) north of Montréal on a peninsula that juts into the Hudson Strait. The Inuit here have adapted to the region's harsh conditions, fashioning a life that pushes against the limitations imposed by the environment. The Nunavik Arctic Survival Training Center offers customized adventure travel itineraries. Contact the center about opportunities to build an igloo in Quaqtaq using traditional tools and methods.

2-DAY ADVENTURE | For a two-day trip to Québec's Far North, travel to Puvirnituq, the largest Inuit town on Hudson Bay's east coast and gateway to the region's more remote settlements. Time your arrival to coincide with the community's snow festival. Held every two years during the last week in March, this six-day celebration of traditional Inuit culture includes snow and ice sculptures, an igloo-building competition, races, and music performances in the evenings. Devote your second day in Puvirnituq to one of Nunavik's quintessential activities: dogsledding. Although the Inuit today largely get around by snowmobile, the dogsled, once essential to the nomadic way of life, is again popular. Many communities offer dogsled tours and races like the Ivakkak. Check with guides in town to see what is on offer.

3-DAY ADVENTURE | Begin in the Inuit town of Salluit, near the Hudson Strait. From August to March the aurora borealis (northern lights) is visible in this region, and, because there is little light pollution in the whole of Nunavik, the sight is spectacular, matched by few other places in the world. While a few hotels and eateries cater to visitors, there is virtually no infrastructure for supporting tourism related to the aurora; so just head outside or ask local residents for advice about the best viewing spots. On day two head to Déception Bay, renowned for hunting and world-class fishing. Note that licenses are required for these activities. Before planning your trip, contact Nunavik's Department of Environment and Canada's Department of Fisheries and Oceans for details about obtaining licenses and for a list of hunting and fishing regulations. Spend day three nearby at narrow Sugluk Inlet, where the wildlife-watching promises to be stellar. Nesting pairs of golden eagles have been spotted here, and Arctic plants abound. Finish back in Salluit with a well-earned dinner at Restaurant Café-Croute.

Outside the village of Puvirnituq, Eric Ittukallak cracks thick ice using a metal pole with a sharp blade. With his fishing line he may catch 11 eel in a few minutes—a feast for himself and his sled dogs.

FAVORITE PLACES

DESTINATIONS IN CANADA'S BEAUTIFUL PROVINCE

Mont Chaudron | Located in Abitibi-Témiscamingue, Mont Chaudron is made of sedimentary rock that formed more than 2.3 billion years ago. Its shape is reminiscent of an upside-down cauldron. (pages 218–219)

Bic National Park | Shaped by strong winds and frozen from intense cold, the shores of Îlet au Flacon—"bottle island"—in Bic National Park, form a winter ice sculpture. (pages 66–67)

Jupiter River | On Île d'Anticosti, in the famous Jupiter 24 pool—one of 30 good fishing pools along the Jupiter River—salmon are easily visible in the crystalline waters. (Île d'Anticosti: pages 14–15, 20–21)

La Grande River | Canoeing in the heart of the taiga, under a sky bursting with color on the Grande River in Eeyou Istchee Baie-James is an unforgettable experience. (page 239)

Abitibi Everglades | Rivers and streams crisscross the wetlands of Lake Parent north of Senneterre, in Abitibi-Témiscamingue. The area is sometimes called Abitibi Everglades. (Abitibi: pages 212–227)

Baie-Saint-Paul | The harmonious blend of evening colors that often drapes the local mountains and St. Lawrence River helps make Baie-Saint-Paul in Charlevoix an inspiration for artists. (pages 97, 103)

Mingan Archipelago | Dotting the islands of Côte-Nord, these limestone monoliths sculpted by the wind and sea evoke wonder among visitors. (page 21)

Trans-Taiga Road | The aurora borealis dances over a Cree camp on the side of the remote Trans-Taiga Road, which leads to the Eeyou Istchee Baie-James region. (pages 238–239)

Pointe-au-Père Lighthouse | Once key to maritime life in Bas Saint-Laurent, Pointe-au-Père is the second tallest lighthouse in Canada and a national historic site. (Bas Saint-Laurent: pages 64–77)

Montmagny | On the south side of the St. Lawrence River, the islands off Montmagny host pleasure craft in the summer. In October, the city welcomes migrating snow geese and the annual Snow Goose Festival. (pages 124–125)

Mont Mégantic National Park | The first light of day creates a muted landscape as it strikes the frozen mountains of this park in Cantons-de-l'Est, home to Mont Mégantic Observatory. (page 146)

Chic-Choc Mountains | During the blue hour, the Chic-Chocs rise majestically on the Gaspésie horizon. The Auberge de Montagne, at 2,017 feet (615 m), blends into the vista. (page 43)

Cap Bon-Ami I At dawn in Forillon National Park in Gaspésie, this landmark is exceptionally beautiful with its sheer cliffs illuminated by the morning light. (page 34)

The Magdalen Islands I Here is a photographer's paradise. The enormous cliffs of Havre-aux-Maisons rise above the beaches and have an almost magical appearance at sunrise. (pages 46–63)

Nunavik I On the vast Arctic desert of Nunavik this stone figure—an *inunnguaq* ("like a human")—looms before a sublime horizon and other natural elements beyond the camera lens. (pages 246–263)

Old Québec I At sunset, the horizon blazes for a few minutes, providing this shot of Old Québec, an image worth a thousand words. (pages 80–82, 106–111)

Dorwin Falls I Lookouts offer stunning views of Dorwin Falls, which cascades from a height of 60 feet (18 m), on the Ouareau River in Chutes Dorwin Park in Lanaudière. (Lanaudière: pages 182–189)

Île du Havre-Aubert I After rain and strong winds, the island's horizon is set alight by golden rays, and the village of La Grave is transformed into a breathtaking scene. (pages 62–63)

Montréal I On a cold January morning, Old Montréal stirs beneath a fog that offers glimpses of the architecture along its riverbank. The heart of Montréal rises in the background. (pages 170–181)

Jacques Cartier National Park I The majestic park's glacial valley is dressed in autumn colors, which emphasize the topography—mountainous plateaus cut by abrupt, sheer-sided valleys. (page 117)

Devil's River I The Escalier rapids churn on Devil's River as it cuts through Mont Tremblant National Park. A choice venue for camping and canoeing, the river also promises still waters and meandering curves. (page 194)

Îles de Boucherville National Park I Near Montréal, this park's lush green spaces and lively channels with pathways bordering the water wait to be discovered by outdoor enthusiasts. (pages 162–163)

Gatineau Park I At the summit of the park's Eardly Escarpment, the Champlain Lookout offers one of the most popular views of the park, which includes the Ottawa River Valley. (pages 205, 209)

Saguenay Fjord I Bright rays of sun fall on Saguenay Fjord—sculpted by ancient ice sheets—near Lake St. John. The effect is both mysterious and dazzling. (pages 84–85, 87)

ACKNOWLEDGMENTS

TO PHOTOGRAPH QUÉBEC for this book has been one of the most rewarding experiences of my life. I traveled more than 43,000 miles (70,000 km) to the heart of territories of sharp contrast. Discovering new landscapes and meeting others who share my deep love of Québec has been a privilege and genuine pleasure. It is not possible in a single page to thank all those who helped and supported me in this journey. Guides, friends, family, co-workers, serendipitous encounters — all are part of the collaboration, the exchanges, and the sharing that have enriched this work and my life. To those whose paths I crossed, I offer my heartfelt gratitude for your judicious counsel and the creative energy you inspired in me.

I would first like to thank Bill O'Donnell, Barbara Brownell Grogan, Patricia Kim-Scott, Jerry Sealy, Moira Haney, Mary Stephanos, and the entire National Geographic team who worked on this project. Thank you for your professionalism, your patience, and your invaluable help in this creative process. It has been an honor to work with you.

A very special thank-you to the team of the Alliance de l'Industrie Touristique du Québec for their support, especially Martin Soucy, Sébastien Viau, Édith Beaulieu, Julia Yaccarini, and Marie-Hélène Hudon. This book would not have been possible without our unique collaboration. I thank the regional tourist associations of Québec for their warm welcome, their generous guidance, and the remarkable support they provided for some special photo shoots. A deep and notable thanks to Le Québec Maritime as well as Tourisme Autochtone Québec and Association des Stations de ski du Québec for our high-level professional relationships. This bond of trust enabled me to deepen my understanding of the St. Lawrence River and the lifestyle of the residents along its shores, as well as the Québec Aboriginal culture. Thanks as well to Parks Canada and Parcs Québec (Sépaq), longtime collaborators with whom I worked to consolidate the photos of historic and natural sites.

I especially thank my mother, Pauline Clermont, for her unwavering commitment to and support in editing this book. Her exceptional work has done justice to my ideas and my words. A thousand thanks to my life partner Milène Cloutier, who demonstrated boundless understanding and support for projects during my months away or who accompanied me as an assistant. Thank you to my father, Luc Dupuis, for our many hours of discussion about the regions of Québec, as well as his invaluable help in readying my "adventure mobile," which provided a truly unique way to experience Québec destinations!

Finally, I am deeply grateful to my equipment partners: GM Canada and Thibault Chevrolet of Rouyn-Noranda, Fibrobec Spacekap, Gosselin Photo, Canon Canada, and Nanuk. Their equipment and products made this journey a reality. These months on the road in search of the perfect light have been an exceptional adventure.

INDEX

Since 1888, the National Geographic Society has funded more than 12,000 research, exploration, and preservation projects around the world. National Geographic Partners distributes a portion of the funds it receives from your purchase to National Geographic Society to support programs including the conservation of animals and their habitats.

National Geographic Partners
1145 17th Street NW
Washington, DC 20036-4688 USA

Get closer to National Geographic explorers and photographers, and connect with our global community. Join us today at nationalgeographic.com/join.

For information about special discounts for bulk purchases, please contact National Geographic Books Special Sales: specialsales@natgeo.com

For rights or permissions inquiries, please contact National Geographic Books Subsidiary Rights: bookrights@natgeo.com

Library of Congress Cataloging-in-Publication Data
Names: Dupuis, Mathieu, author.
Title: Québec : a photographic road trip through Canada's beautiful province
/ Mathieu Dupuis.
Description: Washington, D.C. : National Geographic, [2018] | Includes index.
Identifiers: LCCN 2017041410 | ISBN 9781426219276
Subjects: LCSH: Québec (Province)--Description and travel. | Québec
(Province)--Pictorial works. | Québec (Province)--Guidebooks.
Classification: LCC F1052 .D87 2018 | DDC 917.1404--dc23
LC record available at https://lccn.loc.gov/2017041410

Printed in China

17/PPS/1